Maré from the Inside

Maré from the Inside
Art, Culture and Politics in Rio de Janeiro, Brazil

Edited by
Nicholas Barnes, Desirée Poets and Max O. Stephenson Jr., Eds.

With photographs by Antonello Veneri
and production by Henrique Gomes

Virginia Tech Institute for Policy
and Governance in association with

B L A C K S B U R G ▪ V I R G I N I A

Copyright © 2021 Nicholas Barnes, Desirée Poets and Max O. Stephenson Jr.
Individual chapters © 2021 respective authors
Photographs by Antonello Veneri © 2021 Antonello Veneri

For more information regarding the images photographed by Antonello Veneri and produced by Henrique Gomes, contact Antonello Veneri at antonelloveneri@hotmail.com.

First published 2021 by Virginia Tech Institute of Policy and Governance in association with Virginia Tech Publishing.

Virginia Tech Institute of Policy and Governance
201 West Roanoke St.
Blacksburg, VA 24060

Virginia Tech Publishing
University Libraries at Virginia Tech
560 Drillfield Drive
Blacksburg, VA 24061

This work is licensed under the Creative Commons Attribution-NonCommercial-NoDerivatives 4.0 International License. To view a copy of this license, visit http://creativecommons.org/licenses/by-nc-nd/4.0/ or send a letter to Creative Commons, PO Box 1866, Mountain View, California, 94042, USA. Note to users: This work may contain components (e.g., photographs, illustrations, or quotations) not covered by the license. Every effort has been made to identify these components but ultimately it is your responsibility to independently evaluate the copyright status of any work or component part of a work you use, in light of your intended use. (For further licensing information see pp. xi-xii.)

Cataloging-in-Publication Data

Maré from the inside: art, culture and politics in Rio de Janeiro, Brazil / edited by Nicholas Barnes, Desirée Poets, and Max O. Stephenson Jr; with photographs by Antonello Veneri; with a foreword by James N. Green.

Includes bibliographical references.

ISBN: 978-1-949373-54-7 (paperback - English Edition)
ISBN: 978-1-949373-55-4 (PDF - English Edition)
ISBN: 978-1-949373-56-1 (paperback - Portuguese Edition)
ISBN: 978-1-949373-57-8 (PDF - Portuguese Edition)

DOI: https://doi.org/10.21061/mare

1. PHOTOGRAPHY / Collections, Catalogs, Exhibitions / Group Shows. 2. PHOTOGRAPHY / Photojournalism. 3. SOCIAL SCIENCE / Social Classes & Economic Disparity. 4. SOCIAL SCIENCE / Sociology / Urban. 5. POLITICAL SCIENCE / World / Caribbean & Latin American.
I. Barnes, Nicholas. II. Poets, Desirée. III. Stephenson, Max O. Jr. IV. Veneri, Antonello.

For the Residents of Maré

CONTENTS

Editors' Biographies	ix
Contributors' Biographies	xi
List of Figures	xiii
Foreword *James N. Green*	xvii
Acknowledgments	xxi
Introduction: The Making of *Maré from the Inside* *Nicholas Barnes and Peter Klein*	1
Chapter 1: A Brief History of Rio de Janeiro's Favelas and Complexo da Maré *Nicholas Barnes*	9
Chapter 2: Policing Rio de Janeiro and Complexo da Maré *Nicholas Barnes and Stephanie Savell*	19
Chapter 3: The Portraits of *Maré from the Inside* and their Production *Henrique Gomes*	29
Chapter 4: The Artistic Power of *Maré from the Inside* *Andreza Jorge and Desirée Poets*	37
Chapter 5: Family Constellations and Affective Bonds in *Maré from the Inside* *Molly F. Todd*	45

Chapter 6: Truth-telling, Meaning Making, and Imagining Fresh Possibilities 51
Max O. Stephenson Jr.

Conclusion: On the Struggle for Freedom and Dignity 59
Max O. Stephenson Jr.

Afterword 65

Endnotes 67

EDITORS' BIOGRAPHIES

Nicholas Barnes is a Lecturer at the University of St. Andrews in Scotland. He was previously a Visiting Assistant Professor of Political Science at Grinnell College and a Postdoctoral Fellow at Brown University's Watson Institute for International and Public Affairs. He has conducted 3 years of fieldwork in Rio de Janeiro's favelas and lived in Maré for 18 months from 2013 until 2015. He is currently working on a book project about how and why gangs engage in governance in Rio's favelas. His academic work has been published in *Perspectives on Politics, Current Sociology, Latin American Research Review*, and the *Oxford Research Encyclopedia of Criminology and Criminal Justice*.

Desirée Poets is Assistant Professor of Postcolonial Theory at Virginia Tech's Department of Political Science and Core Faculty of the Alliance for Social, Political, Ethical, and Cultural Thought (ASPECT) PhD Program. Born and raised in Rio de Janeiro, Poets has been working with urban Indigenous and Black (favela and maroon) movements in Brazil's Southeast Region since 2013. Her research focuses on collaborative and critical research methods, settler colonialism, militarization, and questions of race and racism. Her work has been published or is forthcoming in the *Bulletin of Latin American Research, Settler Colonial Studies, Citizenship Studies, Critical Military Studies*, and the *Routledge Handbook of Postcolonial Politics*, among others.

Max O. Stephenson Jr. is Professor of Public and International Affairs and Director of the Institute for Policy and Governance at Virginia Tech. Stephenson's current research has focused on collaborative governance, leadership and democratic politics, arts and community change processes, NGOs and international development, peace building, and humanitarian relief. He is the author or editor of several books, more than 70 refereed articles and book chapters, and 350 commentaries on democratic politics and democratization.

x

CONTRIBUTORS' BIOGRAPHIES

Henrique Gomes is an activist and resident of Complexo da Maré. He coordinates *Maré que Queremos*, a project that brings favela leaders together to improve favela conditions, *Espaço Normal*, a space of refuge for drug users and the homeless, and the *Territorial Development* axis of *Redes de Desenvolvimento da Maré*.

James N. Green is the Carlos Manuel de Céspedes Professor of Latin American History and Professor of Brazilian History and Culture at Brown University. He is the author or co-editor of eleven books on twentieth-century Brazilian history.

Andreza Jorge is a Black feminist, mother, academic, and resident of Complexo da Maré. She has worked with a variety of social projects focused on racial, gender, and sexual identity. Currently, she is a professor in the Department of Corporeal Arts at the Federal University of Rio de Janeiro as well as a researcher in the program of Arts and Scene Studies at the School of Communication.

Peter Klein is Assistant Professor of Sociology and Environmental and Urban Studies at Bard College. His research focuses on public participation, urban and environmental change, and collective action. He has lived and conducted fieldwork throughout Brazil, including Rio de Janeiro and the Amazon. In addition to publishing numerous articles, Klein is author of *Flooded: Development, Democracy, and Brazil's Belo Monte Dam* (under contract with Rutgers University Press) and co-author of *The Civic Imagination: Making a Difference in American Political Life* (Routledge, 2014).

Stephanie Savell is an anthropologist and Senior Research Associate at Brown University's Watson Institute for International and Public Affairs, where she co-directs the *Costs of War* project. Her research focuses on the U.S. post-9/11 wars as well as policing and activism in Rio de Janeiro's favelas, where she has conducted extensive field research since 2008. Savell has published in *PoLAR: Political and Legal Anthropology Review*, *Focaal: Journal of Global and Historical Anthropology*, and *Smithsonian* magazine, among others, and is co-author of *The Civic Imagination: Making a Difference in American Political Life* (Routledge, 2014).

Nadia Sussman is a video journalist with *ProPublica*. She was based in Brazil from 2013 to 2017, where she produced films for *The New York Times*, *BBC*, and *The Wall Street Journal*.

Molly F. Todd is a third-year Ph.D. student in the interdisciplinary ASPECT program at Virginia Tech. Her current work examines border art as a site of counter-hegemonic politics and knowledge production.

Antonello Veneri is an Italian photojournalist who has lived and worked in Brazil since 2009. He has numerous images and articles published in national and international newspapers and magazines, including a 2014 National Geographic Award for Best Feature.

FIGURES

All figures except for the historic photographs (11-17) are published under a CC BY-NC-ND 4.0 license. All maps (figs. 7-10) were created using ArcGIS® software by Esri. (For more information about Esri software, please visit www.esri.com.)

1   Photograph production at *iolabs* in Providence, RI, 2019 (Photo by Nicholas Barnes)
2   *Maré from the Inside* exhibit on display at Bertelsmann Campus Center, Bard College, 2019 (Photo by Nicholas Barnes)
3   *Maré from the Inside* panel at Bertelsmann Campus Center, Bard College, 2019 (Photo by Nicholas Barnes)
4   *Maré from the Inside* collaborators set up the exhibit at the Watson Institute for International and Public Affairs, Brown University, 2019 (Photo by Nicholas Barnes)
5   *Maré from the Inside* exhibit on display at Burling Library, Grinnell College, 2020 (Photo by Nicholas Barnes)
6   *Maré from the Inside* collaborators recording the "Trustees Without Borders" podcast at the VTIPG Community Change Collaborative, Virginia Tech, 2020 (Photo by Desirée Poets)
7   Map of Brazil, 2020 (Map by Nicholas Barnes)
8   Map of Rio de Janeiro's favelas, 2020 (Map by Nicholas Barnes)
9   Map of Rio de Janeiro's zones, 2020 (Map by Nicholas Barnes)
10 Map of Complexo da Maré, 2020 (Map by Nicholas Barnes)
11 The palafitas of Baixa do Sapateiro, 1969 (Photo by Anthony Leeds; used courtesy of Dona Orisina Vieira Archive at the Museum of Maré – CEASM)
12 Aerial photo of Maré, 1979 (Photo used courtesy of Dona Orisina Vieira Archive at the Museum of Maré – CEASM)
13 The first houses of Vila do João, 1981 (Photo used courtesy of the Clarice Peixoto Archive, Museum MIIM)
14 Construction of a new part of Nova Holanda, Complexo da Maré, 1991 (Photo by João Roberto Ripper, used courtesy of the Clarice Peixoto Archive, Museum MIIM)
15 Construction of a new part of Nova Holanda, Complexo da Maré, 1991 (Photo by João Roberto Ripper, used courtesy of the Clarice Peixoto Archive, Museum MIIM)

16	Construction of a new part of Nova Holanda, Complexo da Maré, 1991 (Photo by João Roberto Ripper, used courtesy of the Clarice Peixoto Archive, Museum MIIM)
17	Residents pose in front of their homes, Baixa do Sapateiro, Complexo da Maré, 1981 (Photo used courtesy of the Clarice Peixoto Archive, Museum MIIM)
18	Residents and soldiers watching a Brazil World Cup game during military occupation, Nova Holanda, Complexo da Maré, 2014 (Photo by Antonello Veneri and produced by Henrique Gomes)
19	A soldier hides behind a car during a military operation, Parque Rubens Vaz, Complexo da Maré, 2014 (Photo by Antonello Veneri and produced by Henrique Gomes)
20	Military patrol at dawn on one of Maré's main thoroughfares, Nova Holanda, Complexo da Maré, 2014 (Photo by Antonello Veneri and produced by Henrique Gomes)
21	Spent shell casings discharged by soldiers and collected by a resident, Parque Rubens Vaz, Complexo da Maré, 2014 (Photo by Antonello Veneri and produced by Henrique Gomes)
22	Dona Jurema and her family, Nova Holanda, Complexo da Maré, 2013 (Photo by Antonello Veneri and produced by Henrique Gomes)
23	Dona Tânia Gonçalves and Luiz Carlos, Morro de Timbau, Complexo da Maré, 2014 (Photo by Antonello Veneri and produced by Henrique Gomes)
24	Dona Tânia Gonçalves and Luiz Carlos, Morro de Timbau, Complexo da Maré, 2016 (Photo by Antonello Veneri and produced by Henrique Gomes)
25	Senhor Antônio, Parque Maré, Complexo do Maré, 2013 (Photo by Antonello Veneri and produced by Henrique Gomes)
26	Paulo Victor and Matheus Affonso, Nova Holanda, Complexo da Maré, 2018 (Photo by Antonello Veneri and produced by Henrique Gomes)
27	Eliane Antunes, Herbet Oliveira dos Santos and Adriel Oliveira dos Santos, with dog Pipoca, Nova Holanda, Complexo da Maré, 2014 (Photo by Antonello Veneri and produced by Henrique Gomes)
28	Kelly Santos and Gael Aguiar, Nova Holanda, Complexo da Maré, 2018 (Photo by Antonello Veneri and produced by Henrique Gomes)
29	Vera Marcelino, Parque Maré, Complexo da Maré, 2013 (Photo by Antonello Veneri and produced by Henrique Gomes)
30	Andreza Jorge and Alice Odara, Nova Holanda, Complexo da Maré, 2016 (Photo by Antonello Veneri and produced by Henrique Gomes)

31	Sofia Felicidade and Dona Maria, Parque Maré, Complexo da Maré, 2016 (Photo by Antonello Veneri and produced by Henrique Gomes)
32	Nelson Teixeira with dog, Parque Maré, Complexo da Maré, 2016 (Photo by Antonello Veneri and produced by Henrique Gomes)
33	Two women during a Brazil World Cup game, Nova Holanda, Complexo da Maré, 2014 (Photo by Antonello Veneri and produced by Henrique Gomes)
34	Children playing on a fallen tree game after a storm, Nova Holanda, Complexo da Maré, 2016 (Photo by Antonello Veneri and produced by Henrique Gomes)
35	Residents watch the actions of the Brazilian Armed Forces during the occupation, Parque Rubens Vaz, Complexo da Maré, 2014 (Photo by Antonello Veneri and produced by Henrique Gomes)
36	A woman takes care of her neighbor's daughter, Parque Maré, Complexo da Maré, 2016 (Photo by Antonello Veneri and produced by Henrique Gomes)

FOREWORD

JAMES N. GREEN

In the late 1950s, as President Juscelino Kubitschek celebrated the construction of Brasília, which replaced Rio de Janeiro as the country's new capital, the Franco-Italian-Brazilian feature film *Orfeu Negro* (*Black Orpheus*, 1958) captured the imagination of international audiences. Shot exquisitely in black and white by French Director Marcel Camus with an all-Black cast of actors and set in the favelas of Rio de Janeiro during Carnival, the movie retold the Greek love story of Orpheus and Eurydice. In one of the movie's first scenes, during the preparations for pre-Lenten festivities, dark-skinned women deftly carry cans of water on their heads up the steep slopes of their hillside neighborhoods, transmitting a carefree and happy attitude toward their lives amidst the poverty of their surroundings.

The film's soundtrack opens with António Carlos Jobin's bossa nova classic *Felicidade* (*Happiness*), with lyrics by Vinícius de Moraes declaring: "Tristeza não tem fim. Felicidade sim" ("Sadness has no ending. Happiness does"). Although the film has the catastrophic ending of a Greek tragedy, foreign filmgoers could only be in awe of the glorious views of Rio from atop the granite hills where the city's humble residents dwelled. No doubt, the script's and the cast's seemingly lighthearted approach to life, even as sadness never ends, played a seductive role in ensuring the film's international acclaim. *Black Orpheus* won a Golden Globe and an Oscar for best foreign film in 1960 and became the cinematic postcard image of Rio de Janeiro, which, no doubt, attracted tourists from throughout the world for years to come.

Four decades later, Fernando Meirelles and Kátia Lund's film, *Cidade de Deus* (*City of God*, 2002), offered a stark contrast to that romanticized portrayal of Rio's poor neighborhoods. Loosely based on Paulo Lins' 1997 novel of the same name, the film chronicled the development of organized crime between the 1960s and 1980s in the City of God housing project built in western Rio to house residents removed from favelas overlooking Rio's iconic beaches, much like the one depicted in *Black Orpheus*. Ironically, construction on the housing project began the same year that *Black Orpheus* won international accolades. Nominated for four Academy awards, although not for Best

Foreign Film, many critics consider *City of God* to be one of Brazil's best films of the twentieth century.

The two films, however, could not be more dramatically different as *City of God* replaced the communal collectivity and upbeat social interactions depicted in *Black Orpheus* with violence and murder perpetrated by drug dealers who terrorize the community's residents amid battles for territory with rival gangs and the police. Unfortunately, this is the image of Rio's low-income neighborhoods worldwide today. *Maré from the Inside* challenges these one-dimensional portrayals of the city's poor communities. As such, this book and the Exhibit on which it is based are an important corrective to the way that Rio's favelas are viewed or imagined by people both inside and outside of Brazil.

The power of this volume is the simplicity and sensitivity of the ways its creators have chosen to depict Maré through a series of captivating portraits of its residents set in their homes and neighborhood surroundings. Rather than danger and violence, the images transmit domesticity and humanity. Brightly colored walls and meticulously arranged rugs and furniture reveal that residents take pride in their homes and are at ease in quotidian interactions with family, friends, and neighbors. There are no romantic representations of happy-go-lucky residents, as in Camus' 1958 film. Equally, the violence of gangs, militias, and police repression, while at times present, are not the volume's principal focus.

Moreover, this volume reflects the commitment of its creators to horizontally-based collaborations among U.S. academics, an Italian-Brazilian photographer, and researchers, activists and residents of Maré. How does one actually construct such a project in a manner that does not continue to reproduce the unequal power relations between North and South, white and Black, middle-class and poor? While it is impossible to undermine completely the mechanisms that generate voyeurism towards the Other, it is clear that these authors and collaborators conceived and realized a form of knowledge production that respected the residents of Maré while educating a wider audience to a reality that challenges the stereotypes that most Brazilians and others have of favela residents. The close relationship that Henrique Gomes, a Maré activist and one of the Exhibit's co-creators, has with the residents whose images are captured in this book's photographs, was clearly the foundation on which this project was built. Their mutual trust and collaborative spirit allowed for an intimacy and candidness in the portraits that would have been impossible to capture otherwise.

I had the pleasure of viewing the Exhibit at Brown University. My two favorite portraits were of a couple sitting on a couch in a narrow living room. In the first image (see fig. 23), a set of white cabinets and shelves line one wall with a bulky television and boombox stereo atop, squeezing into a room that is painted a dull green. The second photograph of the same couple on the same couch (see fig. 24), revealed that a large copy of the original portrait had replaced the unwieldy piece of furniture. Bright pink paint covers the room's walls in this photograph giving the space a festive air. Life goes on. The large photograph on the wall documents a fleeting moment in the couple's past. Yet, there is a sense of continuity in their occupation of the room. The picture within the picture elicited an empathetic response on my part as I imagined how pleased the couple must have been when they received this portrait. Still, one cannot sidestep the reality that any viewer of this image ends up voyeuristically gazing on the people they are observing despite the best intentions of the Exhibit's organizers to break down the distinction between those looking in and those being observed.

This dilemma becomes one of the powerful qualities of *Maré from the Inside*, which goes far beyond the flat, though picturesque, portraits of Rio's favelas in *Black Orpheus* and the violence and chaos of *City of God*. The outsider visiting this Exhibit has no real ability to live within and experience Maré or any other favela for that matter. They cannot divest themselves of their privilege simply by looking at these photographs. Yet, this volume and the Exhibit it accompanies provide an opportunity to consider, to reflect, and to develop empathy, which can be powerful emotional as well as intellectual tools for reimagining what is, what could be, and what should be for this community's residents. No single academic or artistic endeavor can overturn the legacies of slavery, exploitation, and marginalization of the mostly African-descendant residents of Rio's favelas. Nor can one reasonably expect that it will be easy to overturn stereotypical images of the poor and working class that have long exoticized or excused on-going poverty and socio-economic inequality. This work, nonetheless, is an act of respect that contributes an alternative understanding of what it means to live and survive in Rio's favelas with dignity and humanity.

February 1, 2021
Providence, Rhode Island

xx

ACKNOWLEDGMENTS

This book and the Exhibit to which it is intimately tied owe their combined existence to the generosity and spirit of Complexo da Maré's residents. All of the artists, activists and academics involved in this collaborative endeavor have been inspired and fascinated by Maré. As such, we first want to thank all of the Complexo's inhabitants, from the first incomers along the marshy banks of Guanabara Bay to the most recent arrivals to the sprawling set of neighborhoods that make up Maré today.

Although we cannot list them all here, we want also to recognize the friends, family members, colleagues and organizations that brought us together and that helped to foster the bonds of friendship and support that made this Exhibit and book a reality. In particular, we would like to thank all of the families of Maré that agreed to join Henrique Gomes and Antonello Veneri in the *Interiores da Maré* project. We are grateful to each of the families for opening their homes and inspiring us to keep on learning, listening, and cultivating knowledge. We also want to thank Eliana Sousa Silva and the rest of the *Redes da Maré* staff and community for the support and encouragement to several of the collaborators.

A special thanks also goes to Francisco Valdean and the Museum of the Itinerant Image of Maré (MIIM) as well as Claudia Rose Ribeiro da Silva and the Museum of Maré for access to their archives and the use of several images.

The idea to produce and exhibit Antonello Veneri and Henrique Gomes' marvelous photography project to audiences beyond Maré first crystallized at Brown University, where Nicholas Barnes was a Postdoctoral Fellow at the Watson Institute for International and Public Affairs. Steven Bloomfield, Associate Director of the Watson Institute encouraged the Exhibit's realization from its first mention and the *Art at Watson Fund* helped make it a financial and logistical reality. *Maré from the Inside* also received generous support from James Green and the Brazil Initiative, the Center for Latin American and Caribbean Studies, the Swearer Center, the Cogut Institute for the Humanities, the Center for the Study of Race and Ethnicity in America, and the Pembroke Center for Teaching and Research on Women at Brown University. Emma Sampson at *iolabs* in East Providence, RI worked diligently to produce high quality and durable photographs. We would also like to thank Sarah Baldwin and Carl Smith for their help in preparing the photographs and other exhibit materials for their public debut.

The initial production of the photographs and the first *Maré from the Inside* events would not have been possible without the support of many programs, centers and individuals at Bard College. At Bard, The Office of Inclusive Excellence, the Center for Civic Engagement, and the Center for the Study of Hate provided generous support. We would also like to thank the Environmental and Urban Studies program, Global and International Studies, Human Rights, Anthropology, Art History, Photography, Political Studies, as well as the Latin and Iberian Studies Concentration. These academic programs provided significant financial support and a great deal of enthusiasm for the project. A special thank you goes to Bard's Sociology Program, whose contributions not only supported *Maré from the Inside*, but also allowed for the purchase of additional photographs so that part of the Exhibit could live on at Bard. We also greatly appreciate the work of Melissa Germano in arranging on-campus event logistics and travel plans for participants.

At Grinnell College, we would like to thank the Political Science Department (especially Gemma Sala, Barb Trish, and Barry Driscoll), the Center for the Humanities, the Rosenfield and Chrystal Funds, as well as Kathryn Patch and Shuchi Kapila at the Institute for Global Engagement. A special note of appreciation goes to Lynn Stafford who helped organize all of the logistics and travel for our participants at Grinnell. *Maré from the Inside*'s presentation at Burling Library would also not have been possible without the support and expertise of Lesley C. Wright, Tilly Woodward, and Milton Severe of the Grinnell College Museum of Art.

The skills, generosity, and support of our colleagues at Virginia Tech have been indispensable to the realization of this project. We would like to thank the Virginia Tech Institute for Policy and Governance, whose Community Change Collaborative continues to be so central to the development of the collaborations behind this project on all levels. The students, staff, and faculty associated with the Collaborative have been a driving force in this work, helping us design, conceptualize, and execute the research to which this project belongs. We also thank the Department of Political Science, the Virginia Tech Center for Humanities, and the College of Liberal Arts and Human Sciences (in particular its International Initiatives Small Grant program) for the logistical, administrative, and financial support they have provided. We are equally grateful to Beatriz Ribeiro Araujo for the professional translation of this book's Preface as well as during other activities throughout the project. *Maré from the Inside* would not be coming to Virginia Tech were it not for the expertise, enthusiasm, and flexibility of Scott Fralin at University Libraries, who is guiding us in our efforts to create an in-person and companion virtual exhibit. This book, in turn, would not have been possible without generous funding from the Virginia Tech Center for Peace Studies and Violence Prevention, which we acknowledge with special thanks. Finally, Virginia Tech Publishing is worthy of special mention. We thank its team, Peter Potter (Director) and Robert Browder (Publishing Specialist), for believing in our project and helping us realize it. Dr. Luysyena Kirakosyan has been an equally invaluable collaborator. Her expertise has made this book's unconventional layout and design possible and she has also kindly helped us with translations from English to Portuguese of chapters 1 and 6. Finally, this book's cover is the creation of Nathalie Poets, whom we thank for her time, generosity, and creativity.

Nicholas Barnes, Desirée Poets,
Max O. Stephenson Jr.
January 4, 2021

INTRODUCTION
THE MAKING OF *MARÉ FROM THE INSIDE*

NICHOLAS BARNES AND PETER KLEIN

Maré from the Inside is an interactive visual and textual exhibit developed through a collaboration among Brazilian and U.S.-based artists, activists and academics. It focuses on the lives of residents in Complexo da Maré, a group of 16 contiguous favelas and housing projects in the Northern Zone of Rio de Janeiro. Situated just a short distance from Rio's international airport and at the confluence of the city's three major highways—Avenida Brasil, the Red Line and the Yellow Line—Maré is Brazil's largest agglomeration of favelas with an estimated population of 140,000 individuals. The community encompasses less than 2 square miles, making it one of the most densely populated places in all of the Americas. It is home to various Afro-descendant populations, migrants from Brazil's impoverished Northeast region and numerous religious and ethnic groups, as well as immigrants from more than 15 countries.

Maré is a vibrant and diverse set of neighborhoods that evidence a variety of forms of cultural and artistic production as well as powerful social movements. The Complexo and its various neighborhoods have also played an important role in the politics of Brazil, gaining international recognition as the birthplace of Marielle Franco, a beloved Rio city councilwoman tragically assassinated in March of 2018. Maré and its residents have also long been ignored by the City's social and political institutions and, thus, much of life in the community is marked by poverty and a lack of infrastructure and social services. Maré has also been subject to repressive policing practices since the community's formation in the early 20th century. This systemic marginalization and discrimination is not inherent to its residents. Rather, Maré is defined by the dynamism, resilience, and permanence of its population.

Why Maré from the Inside?

Maré from the Inside provides views into favela residents' lives that have rarely been captured previously. Its images challenge long-standing and powerful stigmatizing narratives, demonstrating instead the diversity and creativity of these communities and exposing the barriers residents confront in their everyday lives. In the end, the Exhibit profiled in these pages suggests the need for a rethinking of prevailing social frames and for a fresh set of political and cultural strategies capable of breaking the cycles of exclusion and marginalization experienced by favela communities in Brazilian social and political life.

The collective character of *Maré from the Inside* reflects an ongoing effort among those involved to develop more horizontal relations between favela communities in Rio and academic institutions and communities in the Global North. Ultimately, we view such projects as necessary to decolonize and democratize Northern academic institutions.

Who are Maré from the Inside's Creators?

Artists. Researchers. Scholars. Activists. Teachers. Organizers. Journalists. *Maré from the Inside* arose from a series of personal and professional relationships among people with very different identities, backgrounds and perspectives. Henrique Gomes and Andreza Jorge are lifelong residents of Maré. They are both Black activists, have worked for several nonprofit organizations, and are deeply committed to improving conditions in their community. Stephanie Savell, Nicholas Barnes, and Peter Klein are researchers based in the United States and Scotland who study security, local governance, and urban inequality in Brazil. The relationships among Gomes, Jorge, and these researchers began in 2008 with informal conversations between Jorge and Savell.

In 2012, Savell and Barnes were Ph.D. students engaged in long-term fieldwork in Maré and surrounding favelas. Gomes, a cultural producer, provided each with invaluable local knowledge and guidance for conducting ethical, safe, and culturally sensitive research in Maré. As the relationships among these individuals deepened, the character of Savell and Barnes' research projects evolved. The pair became more critical of existing inquiries concerning favelas and each sought to engage and incorporate Maré's residents more fully into their work. Ultimately, the research the three individuals carried out together and the friendship they developed during this period provided the foundation from which *Maré from the Inside* emerged.

Gomes has since supported dozens of researchers and journalists as they sought to conduct studies in Maré. Not only has his assistance improved their work, but he has, in most cases, been crucial in making their projects possible. Antonello Veneri was one such person with whom Gomes has collaborated. Veneri is an Italian photojournalist who has lived and worked in Brazil since 2011. Veneri was engaged in a long-term photography project in 2013 when he partnered with Gomes. Their initial idea was to take family portraits of Maré residents "inside" their homes to show a side of favela life rarely captured for external audiences and also to revive a tradition of portraiture that many of Maré's residents brought with them as migrants from the Northeast of Brazil. During the course of two years, Gomes and Veneri worked with more than 30 families to create intimate and accurate portraits that present their subjects in a respectful and non-fetishized way while also capturing Maré's remarkable diversity.

Most of the family portraits were taken during a particularly turbulent period in the community's history. Beginning in April 2014, just before the start of the World Cup, as outlined in chapter 2, Maré was occupied by 2,500 soldiers as part of a public security program called "Pacification" designed to retake control of Rio's militia and drug gang-dominated favelas. Barnes was conducting ethnographic research in Maré during this period and was able to participate in the photography project as Veneri and Gomes worked with families across Maré. By traveling to every corner of the Complexo, the artists simultaneously documented daily life on the streets, the reality of occupation and the stresses placed on community relations and identities during this significant and difficult period. The juxtaposition of the two sets of photographs—from inside and outside the homes of Maré's residents—offer complementary perspectives from which to view favela life and identity.

During the same period, Gomes also worked with Nadia Sussman, an American video journalist based in Brazil from 2013 to 2017. Sussman and Gomes, along with several other local artists, produced three short documentary films featured in the Exhibit: *Occupation*,[1] *Girl's Life*,[2] and *Headbanging in the House of God*.[3] Like their photographic counterparts, these films depict daily life on the streets of Maré and wrestle with questions related to race, religion, and violence. Finally, the Exhibit includes essays by Jorge, Savell, and Barnes.

How has this Collaborative Project Evolved?

The idea for *Maré from the Inside* came to life after much of the research comprising it was complete, the photographs taken, and the videos produced. The team raised funds to print a selection of the photographs professionally (see fig. 1) so they could be exhibited. To date, the opening or closing of *Maré from the Inside* at each hosting institution has been accompanied by a series of events featuring both the U.S. and Brazilian-based collaborators. The team adopted this approach with great success at Bard College, Brown University, and Grinnell College.

The first public sharing of the Exhibit opened to the public on January 31, 2019 at Bard College's Bertelsmann Campus Center (see fig. 2). Several hundred students were able to interact with the collaborators when they visited Bard for a series of public presentations, panels, and workshops at the end of February, 2019 (see fig. 3). *Maré from the Inside* then moved to Brown University's Watson Institute for International and Public Affairs, where the team once again had the opportunity to share their experiences and perspectives with hundreds of Brown students and staff as well as members of the larger Providence community (see fig. 4). The most recent public showing of *Maré from the Inside* occurred at Grinnell College's Burling Library from November of 2019 to February of 2020 (see fig. 5). At all three institutions, the collaborators spoke to classes on Latin American politics and history, urban planning and development,

Figure 1. Photograph production at *iolabs* **in Providence, RI, 2019 (Emma Sampson pictured).**

Figure 2. *Maré from the Inside* **Exhibit on display at Bertelsmann Campus Center, Bard College, 2019.**

Figure 3. *Maré from the Inside* panel at Bertelsmann Campus Center, Bard College, 2019. Pictured (from left) are Klein, Gomes, Jorge, Veneri and Savell.

Figure 5. *Maré from the Inside* exhibit on display at Burling Library, Grinnell College, 2020.

Figure 4. *Maré from the Inside* collaborators set up the exhibit at the Watson Institute for International and Public Affairs, Brown University, 2019. Pictured (from left) are Gomes, Veneri, Carl Smith and Sarah Baldwin.

Figure 6. *Maré from the Inside* collaborators (Gomes and Jorge) recording the "Trustees Without Borders" podcast at the VTIPG Community Change Collaborative Virginia Tech, 2020.

colonialism, race and the arts, as well as to students interested in public security and informal economies. The group also ate meals with students, met with faculty, and attended other events on each campus.

Savell, Barnes, and Klein shared some of the insights from their research at events, but primarily served as interpreters for Jorge and Gomes. The group used consecutive interpretation, which meant that Gomes and Jorge spoke a few sentences in Portuguese before pausing to allow another member of the team to translate their thoughts into English. This approach proved effective. Audience members not only heard the perceptions and thoughts of lifelong Maré residents, but also gained a better sense of the speakers' emotions and intentions. Those attending these events also had an opportunity to reflect on powerful statements, such as when Gomes remarked, "I have been in the United States for 21 days and that means it has been 21 days without hearing gunshots," or when Jorge stated, "It is important to recognize that this project is not just about giving voice to communities, because everyone has a voice. This project is an opportunity to listen. We must open spaces and pathways for favela residents to be truly heard."

That same year, Gomes and Jorge visited Virginia Tech, where they were part of several well-attended gatherings, a podcast interview, and a roundtable on "Placing Appalachia and Rio de Janeiro in Dialogue: Arts, Public Health, and Community Organizing" (see fig. 6). This visit took place at the invitation of Desirée Poets, who had met Gomes while conducting fieldwork in Maré the year before, and with the support and collaboration of Max Stephenson Jr. and the Institute for Policy and Governance's Community Change Collaborative. The group decided to bring the Exhibit to Virginia Tech and so, its next stop will be Virginia Tech's Newman Library, which, responding to the constraints of the COVID-19 pandemic, will not only mount *Maré from the Inside* physically, but also share it in a virtual format. The present volume arose from these latest efforts. Its development illustrates how, as the Exhibit has traveled to new locations, it has assumed new forms, deepened and expanded the links that initially formed it, and connected Maré to new places and populations.

In the end, *Maré from the Inside* shares its story in a different way than most Americans are used to experiencing. Each component of the project—its photographs, films, texts, related events, and now, this book—disrupts expected ways of sharing knowledge, particularly in the academy. This effort showcases the voices of those who have always been speaking and writing, as subjects of their own stories and histories, but who are typically the subjects of study, at best, and often the target of disdain and discrimination, at worst.

How is the Book Organized?

This book is divided into two sections. The first addresses the evolution of Complexo da Maré to contextualize *Maré from the Inside*. Barnes traces the historical trajectory of Rio de Janeiro's favelas and Complexo da Maré in chapter 1 by describing their origins and development. Chapter 2, by Barnes and Savell, describes the highly repressive and increasingly militarized policing practices the Brazilian government has employed in its efforts to contain and eradicate these communities and the various criminal groups that operate within them. Gomes details the process by which he and Veneri worked with several dozen families to produce the Exhibits' portraits in chapter 3.

The second section of the volume explores the meaning making processes embedded in this collaborative project. chapter 4, authored by Jorge and Poets, examines four family portraits and analyzes how they challenge hegemonic discourses of gender, sexuality, race, class, family, and affection. In chapter 5, Molly Todd reflects on several conversations she had with Jorge, who was also photographed for the Exhibit, to highlight the universal themes revealed by the lived experience of a Maré resident. Such themes, she shows, challenge stereotypical and Othering representations of favela communities and their residents. Max Stephenson Jr. then considers what the Exhibit conveys concerning the daily lived realities of Maré residents and what those portend for their capacities to challenge and promote change in the dominant and oppressive social imaginary they confront in chapter 6. The book concludes with Max Stephenson Jr. highlighting the vibrancy and ongoing efforts of Maré residents to address the Othering and oppression with which they live to create purpose-filled lives.

Why is the Book in English and Portuguese?

We have chosen to present companion English and Portuguese texts because doing so reflects our collaborative process in this project which, we hope, speaks not only to U.S. audiences, but also to Brazilian ones. All translations are our own, but we stress that neither of the volumes is the "original text" and the other the "translation." Some chapters were written first in English, some in Portuguese, and others simultaneously in both languages. When translating, we followed a "fidelity to the reader" approach, adapting the original text whenever necessary to ensure its intelligibility. We also understand the process of translation as not simply transforming text into another language, but also as a political act that requires us constantly to reevaluate our assumptions concerning social relations, ideologies, and power. The Exhibit and this book were made possible by the distinct—albeit shifting—institutional, professional, socio-economic, geographical, linguistic, and cultural locations of the collaborators, as described above. We hope the present volume both reflects and adequately conveys that layered reality.

CHAPTER 1
A BRIEF HISTORY OF RIO DE JANEIRO'S FAVELAS AND COMPLEXO DA MARÉ

NICHOLAS BARNES

Rio de Janeiro is Brazil's second largest city (behind only São Paulo) and is located in the Southeast region of the country (see fig. 7). The city contains more than 1,000 favelas (see fig. 8) that are home to more than 20% of the city's 6.7 million inhabitants.[1] Although favelas are often referred to as slums, shantytowns, or squatter settlements, these terms fail to capture the incredible diversity among these communities or the significant development that they have undergone during the last century. This chapter provides important social and historical context for the *Maré from the Inside* exhibit and the rest of the chapters in this volume by tracing the origins, growth, and development of Rio's favelas generally, and the 16 favelas and housing projects that comprise Complexo da Maré, more specifically. It also describes the various ways that Maré's residents have organized and advocated for recognition and rights in the face of an often

Figure 7. Map of Brazil, 2020. (Data from ESRI, Garmin, GEBCO, NOAA NGDC and other contributors.)

hostile, negligent, and/or repressive Brazilian state.

Rio de Janeiro: City of Favelas

According to popular myth, Rio de Janeiro's first favela was founded in the 1890s when

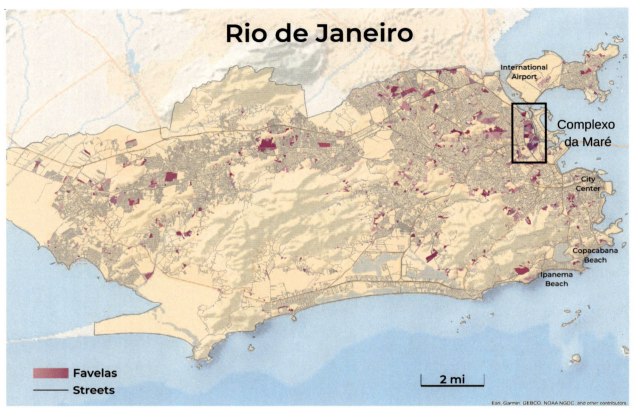

Figure 8. Map of Rio de Janeiro's favelas, 2020. (Data from Instituto Pereira Passos.)

a group of former slaves and ex-soldiers established a community of tents and ramshackle huts on a hill overlooking the city center. They called it *Morro da Favella* (Favella Hill) after a plant that grew in Northeast Brazil where the soldiers had fought in the Canudos War.[2] The actual birth of *Morro*, however, occurred several years earlier following the destruction of *Cabeça do Porco* (Pig's Head), a *cortiço* (tenement) in the center of the city. After authorities razed the massive development, residents gathered what few belongings and building materials they could save and began constructing homes on a nearby hillside.[3] The ex-soldiers joined those first inhabitants at that location several years later.

Emancipated slaves constructed many of Rio's earliest favelas in a similar fashion. Brazil was the last country in the Americas to abolish slavery and was, by far, the world's largest importer of slaves with an estimated 5 million enslaved Africans arriving to its shores during the roughly 300 years of the Trans-Atlantic trade.[4] Rio de Janeiro alone saw more than 2 million such individuals pass through its port. Following the abolition of slavery in 1888, many of the newly freed migrated to Rio and to São Paulo and Belo Horizonte, two other rapidly industrializing cities of Brazil's Southeast region. As in the nation's rural areas, freedmen and freedwomen had little access to land or suitable housing, so they built their homes on the steep hillsides surrounding the city's port and central district. Difficult terrain though it was, over time, these settlements grew from a smattering of huts and shacks into substantial communities with hundreds of domiciles and thousands of residents. Despite government efforts to eradicate these earliest favelas, they continued to grow.

By the early 20th century, however, it was no longer just freedmen and freedwomen who built these communities. Wealthy land speculators, politicians, lawyers, the middle class, traditional rural poor, foreign immigrants and farmers seeking land to raise crops and livestock, among many others, all engaged in land invasions and squatting to acquire a share of Rio's highly valuable real estate.[5] Whereas the first favelas were constructed on the steep almost uninhabitable hillsides overlooking the city center, many of these newer settlements occupied defunct estates, unused church and state properties, virgin land, and even swamps and tidal plains to the north. The Northern Zone, as it came to be called, quickly outpaced the other areas of the city in terms of favela development due to the rapid industrialization of the region, its piecemeal property laws and zoning restrictions, as well as the construction of rail lines and eventually highways connecting Rio to the surrounding areas.

Today, many of these Northern Zone favelas, like their predecessors in the Center and Southern Zone, have gained some modicum of access to often inadequate utilities and services as a result of persistent community organizing and hard-won political mobilization. Most homes in these older favelas have running water and electricity and many of these neighborhoods also have schools and health centers. Some have paved sidewalks and a few even have recreational spaces. Favela streets are alive with local commerce, motorcycles, and foot traffic. Houses in these communities range from very simple shacks in the poorest areas to beautifully tiled multi-story homes replete with modern appliances.

Figure 9. Map of Rio de Janeiro's zones, 2020. (Data from Instituto Pereira Passos.)

Rio's newest favelas have emerged in the sprawling Western Zone of the city, where land remains relatively plentiful (see fig. 9). Unlike their older counterparts, many of these communities lack even the most basic urban infrastructure and services. And yet, despite the difficulties of living in these neighborhoods and the lengthy daily commutes residents endure to reach working class jobs located elsewhere in the city, favelas continue to grow and to be built in the Western Zone.

Overall, favelas constitute an extraordinarily diverse set of communities. What continues to unite them, however, is the fact that their residents remain targets of prejudice and discrimination. Mainstream Brazilian society largely continues to portray favelas as areas of vice and criminality.[6] As the *Maré from the Inside* exhibit suggests, however, this cultural frame is a fallacy. Favelas are instead sites of dynamic artistic and cultural production and collective mobilization. Favela artists and musicians are vital to broader cultural representations—they are at the heart, for instance, of Brazil's famed Carnival and samba music—mixing African, European, and indigenous religious and cultural expressions.[7] These communities have also developed self-governing responses to address their residents' lack of property rights and infrastructure. Favela-spawned social movements also played an important role in the popular mobilizations that brought an end to the military dictatorship (1964–1985) and launched Brazil's re-democratization. Today, favelas remain economic and cultural engines. They also sustain vital political and social movements while playing a significant role in the city and nation by advocating for the basic human rights of all of Brazil's citizens.

The Origins of Complexo da Maré

A closer examination of the origins and historical development of Complexo da Maré further demonstrates the diversity and resilience of these communities and thereby challenges long lasting pejorative frames for understanding favelas and their residents. At the end of the 1930s, Orosina Vieira and her husband built a tiny shack out of driftwood on a small hill surrounded by swampy lowlands

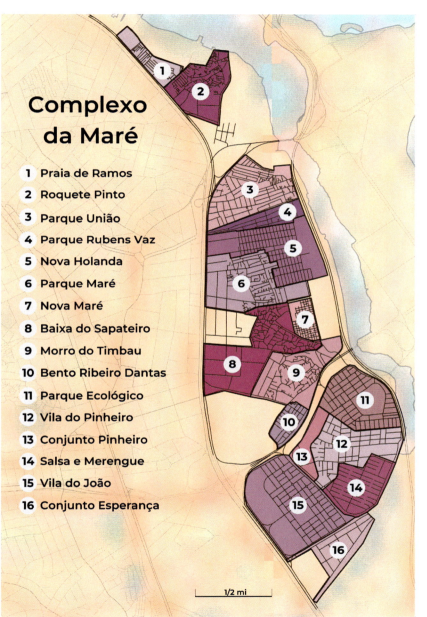

Figure 10. Map of Complexo da Maré (2020). (Data from *Redes de Desenvolvimento da Maré*, ESRI, Garmin, GEBCO, NOAA NGDC and other contributors.)

along Guanabara Bay.[8] The couple, from the neighboring state of Minas Gerais, were Maré's first permanent residents. At that time, the area was completely unsettled except for a colony of fishermen who used it to tie their boats up at night.[9] Slowly, other immigrants followed and by 1940, a small community had taken shape on *Morro do Timbau* (Timbau Hill). This new settlement became Maré's first favela.

In 1946, the national government completed Avenida Brasil, a major highway connecting the center of Rio to surrounding suburbs, and the relative ease of access it provided spurred additional migration to the area. Industries quickly followed and many of Maré's original inhabitants found steady, if often grueling, work in the new factories. Three other communities quickly sprang up in the surrounding area: *Baixa do Sapateiro* (1947), *Parque Maré* (1950) and *Roquete Pinto* (1955). When all of the dry land had been settled, other migrants began to build *palafitas*, or shacks on stilts, further and further out onto the tidal plain of Guanabara Bay (see fig. 10). These were difficult places to live because of their location at or below sea level, without a source of freshwater and due to various water-borne insects and diseases. To address this precarity and to provide much needed electricity and sanitation, these families founded some of the city's first Residents' Associations and Light Commissions.[10]

Parque Rubens Vaz (1954) and *Parque União* (1958), Maré's next two communities, followed a slightly different and more organized pattern of settlement. Margarino Torres, a lawyer and a member of the Communist Party, arrived in Maré in the mid-1950s to protect the fledgling Rubens Vaz favela from threats of removal and he quickly became that community's undisputed leader.[11] He would eventually organize the occupation of an adjacent area, later named Parque União, where a local industrial firm, IRAL, had already filled in some low-lying swampland.[12]

The early 1960s saw the creation of two other communities in Maré. A small group of fishermen settled *Praia de Ramos* (1962) and the municipal government constructed *Centro de Habitação Provisório Nova Holanda* (1962), a provisional housing project. Rio's government initially established Nova Holanda to serve as a stepping-stone to more formal housing for residents who had been violently removed from other favelas in the city. The municipal authority built hundreds of conjoined single- and two-story wood homes, most with dirt floors and no electricity in Nova Holanda (see fig. 11). What was intended to be a "temporary solution," however, turned into a permanent settlement. While each of these neighborhoods retained their distinctive characteristics, residents increasingly moved, shopped, worked, attended school, and developed extended families across

Figure 11. The palafitas of Baixa do Sapateiro, 1969.

Figure 12. Aerial photo of Maré, 1979. Notice the palafitas reaching out into Guanabara Bay in the foreground and the checkerboard streets of Nova Holanda in the background.

their borders. They increasingly identified themselves as part of the overarching community that came to be known as Complexo da Maré.

Life progressively became more difficult in Maré during Brazil's military dictatorship (1964-1985). Continued in-migration led to a swelling population and with very little investment in public infrastructure, the living conditions for many of the Complexo's residents deteriorated. Some 68,000 residents lived in Maré's nine existing communities in 1980, just 40 years after the first area's first inhabitants had arrived.[13] At that time, roughly a quarter of the Complexo's population lived in palafitas, which generally consisted of one room with little or no access to potable water, indoor plumbing or electricity.[14] Residents connected their homes via a series of precariously constructed planks (see fig. 11), which led to many accidents, sometimes proving fatal when small children fell into the water or the mud below.[15]

In 1979, the federal government announced Project Rio, a massive public works initiative, which aimed to fill in huge portions of Guanabara Bay and create 2,300 hectares (5,681 acres) of new land to provide space for housing for an estimated 1.2 million people.[16] At first, the plan called for the eradication of all of the existing communities of Maré. Residents immediately mobilized and created the Committee for the Defense of the Favela of Maré (CODEFAM) to defend their right to stay.[17] After much protest and advocacy, the national administration agreed to allow Maré's existing communities to remain, even as it relocated the families living in the palafitas to a group of newly constructed housing projects just south of Maré: *Vila do João* (1982) (see fig. 12), *Conjunto Esperança* (1982), *Vila do Pinheiro* (1983) and *Conjunto Pinheiro* (1989).[18] These neighborhoods remained part of Maré and would later be joined by several additional housing projects: *Bento Ribeiro Dantas* (1992), *Nova Maré* (1995), and *Salsa e Merengue* (2000) (see fig. 13). All of Maré's communities have continued to grow during the last several decades as new arrivals have undertaken additional construction and claimed available land (see figs. 14, 15, 16). The powerful social movements and mobilizations of the 1970s and 1980s that allowed Maré's various neighborhoods to consolidate have provided

Figure 13. The first houses of Vila do João, 1981.

fertile ground for the development of a diverse and robust organizational environment. Maré is now home to dozens of local NGOs that provide a variety of educational, cultural, and artistic opportunities. Moreover, each of Maré's 16 Residents' Associations continue to offer opportunities for democratic self-governance and to ensure citizen access to much needed social services through the municipal government. Today, Maré is composed of a rich mosaic of ethnic, racial, and religious communities. Indeed, hundreds of religious communities including Evangelical, Catholic, Afro-Brazilian, Asian, and secular traditions can be found in the Complexo. Maré also contains migrants from every one of Brazil's 27 states and from 15 foreign countries as well. It is, and has always been, a melting pot whose existence embodies the progressive and egalitarian ideals at the foundation of Brazilian democracy.

Figures 14, 15, 16. The construction of a new part of Nova Holanda, 1991.

CHAPTER 2
POLICING RIO DE JANEIRO AND COMPLEXO DA MARÉ

NICHOLAS BARNES AND STEPHANIE SAVELL

The Brazilian government has targeted Rio de Janeiro's favelas with repression and violence since their formation. Over the years, the city's public security apparatus has destroyed hundreds of such communities and employed increasingly militarized policing tactics to control and contain their residents. This chapter traces the evolution of those practices to illuminate some of the extraordinary challenges that Maré and other favela residents face in their everyday lives.

Police Repression in Rio de Janeiro

Rio de Janeiro's police regularly extort, harass, imprison, and kill favela residents, who have little recourse to protect themselves from such abusive and corrupt behavior. This has been true since before the first favelas sprang up on the city's steep hillsides. Beginning in the early nineteenth century, Brazil developed police institutions to protect social elites while repressing Black, poor, and immigrant populations, including the persecution of the Black working-class tradition of *capoeira* (dance-like martial arts fighting) and practitioners of Afro-Brazilian religions.[1] At the beginning of the twentieth century, Rio's police targeted urban Black and poor individuals as threats to the "moral, hygienic, and civilizational order" of the city.[2] During Brazil's military dictatorship (1964-1985), this trend intensified as the regime sought to remove favelas and their inhabitants from the city's landscape. From 1968 to 1975 alone, the city of Rio demolished 70 favelas, displacing more than 100,000 residents.[3]

Rio's war on drugs has provided the most recent rationale for repression of Black and working-class residents.[4] Illicit groups formed in most of the city's favelas before the end of the dictatorship; they robbed banks, orchestrated kidnappings and trafficked in illegal drugs. The draconian regime and a deep economic recession that began in the early 1980s dramatically expanded those illegal groups.[5] At the same time, cocaine arrived on the scene, linking these entities to international markets of drugs and heavy weapons, which they acquired to protect their activities.[6] Gradually, as members of these groups were incarcerated, they became integrated into one of the emerging prison-based networks or "factions"—the Red Command (*Comando Vermelho*), the Third Command (*Terceiro Comando*) and, later, Friends of Friends (*Amigos dos Amigos*). These factions, born out of the terrible conditions in Rio's prisons,[7] expanded their power by taking control of numerous favelas, placing residents at the epicenter of a literal and symbolic war between the three factions as well as with state forces.

The militarization of policing in Rio has only intensified since Brazil's re-democratization in the mid-1980s. When police enter trafficker-controlled favelas, they behave like soldiers in enemy territory, seeking to capture or, more often, kill drug dealers, conducting raids on houses, and using armored vehicles and aircraft to support their efforts. Favela residents live in constant fear of the police and the gun battles in which they engage with faction members that all too often kill bystanders, including children.[8]

Notably, police largely ignore the violent and illegal behavior of militias, another set of favela-based armed groups mostly composed of retired and off-duty police and firefighters. Although militias are also violent and profit from extorting businesses and monopolizing illegal transportation, television, internet, and local property markets, Rio police have, for the most part, maintained collaborative and mutually beneficial relationships with them.[9] Today, militias control more favelas than all three drug factions combined.[10]

In 2009, the Rio state government launched an ambitious and controversial policing program, "Pacification," to reestablish state dominance in trafficker-controlled favelas. Couched in discourses of democratic police reform, Police Pacification Units (UPPs) were part of an effort to "clean up" favela neighborhoods in advance of the 2014 World Cup and 2016 Olympic Games. In the first stage of Pacification, police and federal soldiers conducted massive assaults on faction-controlled territories. They then occupied the neighborhoods, engaging in weeks or months of sweeps to find any remaining drugs, weapons and armed group members. This effort was supposed to be followed by the installation of permanent community policing units, UPPs, staffed by newly hired police trained in human rights protocols, to protect and engage favela residents through social programs.

In the early years of pacification, violence across the city dropped sharply, leading many Rio residents to hope that the program might meet its official goals. Yet as the number of UPPs expanded, the Rio police abandoned or never fully implemented rights-based community policing. In 2013, UPP police tortured and executed Amarildo de Souza, a bricklayer in the favela of Rocinha. This shocking event and a subsequent cover-up attempt, sparked massive protests throughout Rio and revealed that the UPP's were continuing to engage in abuse with impunity. Public confidence in Pacification quickly deteriorated following this episode. Then, following the conclusion of the 2016 Olympics, Rio teetered on the edge of bankruptcy and required massive federal bailouts to pay its employees, including police. The Rio government all but abandoned the UPP program thereafter.

The city has since experienced a fresh wave of violence in the last several years. In 2018, Rio police killed 1,534 citizens (a record), only to surpass that number in 2019 by killing 1,814 residents.[11] By comparison, in the entire United States, police killed 992 citizens in 2018 and 999 in 2019.[12] Mounting evidence suggests that local police extra-judicially execute many young Black men they suspect of being drug traffickers, acting on the basis of a virulent racism.[13] Brazil's current president, Jair Bolsonaro, sworn in at the beginning of 2019, along with Rio's governor, Wilson Witzel, have each argued that "criminals" do not deserve the same rights as other citizens and have encouraged even more violent and repressive policing practices in favelas.[14] As a result, police killings have continued to escalate.

Policing Maré

From its earliest days, Maré's relationship to Rio de Janeiro's police and the nation's military has been fraught. As we noted above, the area's first settlers faced almost continuous threats of removal and were regularly harassed and extorted by elements of both of these entities.[15] From the 1940s to the 1960s, some soldiers from an adjacent military base illegally charged residents of *Morro do Timbau* a fee for living in the area and destroyed any homes that were constructed without their approval.[16] Police also had nearly complete discretion concerning the continued existence of these communities. Indeed, local police units engaged in periodic removals of local residents from the 1950s to 1980s (see fig. 17), even razing several entire communities in and around Maré, including Praia de Inhaúma, Maria Angu, Moreninha, and Favela Avenida Brasil.[17] After their homes were demolished or burned, many families fled to surrounding areas to rebuild.

As we highlighted above, repressive police behavior increased markedly during

Figure 17. Residents pose in front of their homes. In the foreground, notice the remnants of another house, demolished by police. Baixa do Sapateiro, Complexo da Maré, 1981.

Brazil's military dictatorship. The regime implemented Institutional Act number 5 in 1968, which suspended some civil and political rights, including *habeas corpus*. Thereafter, police posts located in several areas of Maré began to engage in ever more arbitrary and indiscriminate violence against favela populations. Residents recall many young men being arrested, imprisoned, and in some cases tortured, for supposed "vagrancy" or unemployment. As Eliana Sousa Silva, a local NGO director and community leader has recalled:

> Back then, I saw a lot of young men—even young women—being imprisoned and, sometimes, beaten. There were so many screams and swear words that at times they didn't let us sleep. I

didn't understand, at that time, why they were imprisoned, why they were arrested, and why there was so much misunderstanding and disrespect between the police and the residents.[18]

Like many other favelas across the city, Maré's first drug trafficking and criminal groups formed during the dictatorship. Initially, they were small bands of young men engaged in marijuana sales or armed robbery. With the arrival of cocaine in the 1980s, however, they expanded their organizations and activities, recruiting new members, purchasing more weapons, and competing with one another for control of Maré's valuable turf. In the 1980s and 1990s, Maré's traffickers engaged in frequent shootouts in and amongst homes and businesses as they consolidated their control in those neighborhoods. Eventually, the more successful local groups were incorporated into the Red and Third Command factions. One of Maré's local groups would later shift their allegiance to the third faction, Friends of Friends, in the early 2000s. Finally, a militia took control of the Roquete Pinto and Praia de Ramos neighborhoods in the mid-2000s. Competition among these groups continues to foment local violence to this day.

While Maré's criminal groups are a danger to residents, many of the community's citizens are ambivalent about their presence and role in favela life. Even as they engage in violence and deal in illegal goods, the factions and the militia support local businesses, settle disputes among residents, and implement a relatively stable, if coercive, form of social order by punishing theft, interpersonal violence, and other criminal acts. While most residents disapprove of these groups' violent and illegal activities, they have limited options to resist their presence. Traffickers and militia members alike threaten retribution against residents who report their activities. At the same time, and for obvious reasons, community members have little faith in Rio's violent and corrupt police force.

Maré is a notable example of the militarization of Rio's police that has occurred since the transition to democracy. In the 1990s, police began using armored vehicles to conduct anti-trafficking operations during which they would sometimes engage in violent gun battles with members of the factions, threatening the lives of residents. In 2003, the state installed the 22nd Police Battalion in Nova Holanda, which could rapidly deploy into Maré's other neighborhoods. The Battalion's presence, however, did little to quell the violence among the factions or reduce their power or authority. Then, in 2011, a special forces battalion, BOPE (akin to a Special Weapons and Tactics team, SWAT, in the United States) moved its headquarters to an abandoned military base just outside Maré. For the next several years, BOPE engaged in

Figure 18. Residents and soldiers watching a Brazil World Cup game during military occupation. Nova Holanda, Complexo da Maré, 2014.

frequent operations throughout Maré. In one such effort in June 2013, police confronted a group of traffickers in a brief shootout that resulted in the death of a sergeant. BOPE responded by invading and occupying several of Maré's neighborhoods for the next 24 hours. Police went from house to house searching for faction members, shouting threats from the streets, and eventually killed nine residents, some of whom had little or no connection with drug trafficking.[19] Local NGOs, social movements, and hundreds of Maré residents protested these killings by stopping traffic on Avenida Brasil and demanding accountability. Despite such public outcry, the government did not change its policing practice, nor did it impose any penalties for the abuses that had been committed.

Figure 19. A soldier hides behind a car during a military operation. Parque Rubens Vaz, Complexo da Maré, 2014.

Military Occupation

Complexo da Maré was slated to be the last area of the city "pacified," but the state government never formally implemented community policing or installed a UPP there. Instead, then Brazilian President Dilma Rousseff authorized the occupation of Maré by 2,500 Brazilian military troops from April 2014 to July 2015.[20] Following months of intensive raids intended to weaken Maré's factions, the military stormed the community at dawn on April 5, 2014. The short film, *Occupation*, part of the *Maré from the Inside* exhibit, documents life in Maré on the eve of the military's arrival. It questions the unspoken assumption of favelas as inherently violent spaces that require the Brazilian military's presence. One of the film's most poignant moments occurs during a samba show, when the DJ remarks:

Figure 20. Military patrol at dawn on one of Maré's main thoroughfares. Nova Holanda, Complexo da Maré, 2014.

We are here to show that Maré is not only what they show on the TV. They only show drugs and violence, man. They only show strange things. This place has so many good things and yet that is all they show. We are here to show the good things. ...We are here to show our culture, our art.[21]

The military installed numerous checkpoints at which soldiers stopped and searched residents, especially young Black men. For the duration of the ensuing 16-month occupation, troops conducted 24-hour mobile patrols in which trucks and jeeps monitored the major thoroughfares while soldiers on foot pursued suspicious individuals down Maré's labyrinth of alleyways and narrow side streets (see figs. 18, 19). At night, the military replaced trucks and jeeps with tanks (see fig. 20). While the homicide rate decreased during occupation, due to fewer violent confrontations between the factions and with police, residents nevertheless accused the military of committing a range of abuses.

Troops unlawfully invaded homes and verbally and physically assaulted residents.[22] Soldiers also shot and killed several residents (see fig. 21) who had no known involvement with illegal groups.[23]

Meanwhile, the military engaged in a "hearts and minds" campaign to gain the support of Maré's residents in their efforts to uproot the factions. They allowed municipal workers and construction teams access to Maré for infrastructure upgrading, they organized worship services with local congregations and taught classes addressing maternal health, painting, music, and Jiu-jitsu. Troops offered job training and skills workshops, gave presentations on hygiene and health at local schools, and even organized music concerts. Despite these efforts, by the end of the occupation, less than 25% of 1,000 residents surveyed by Redes da Maré, a local NGO, said the military had behaved well while occupying the community.[24] According to one community leader at a public meeting:

> The "Pacification" of Maré was a lie and an abstract term that doesn't reflect the reality. ... They [the military] haven't implemented more responsive institutions and although they have sought out civil society to develop relationships, this is more in theory and serves as a subterfuge for them to control the space. (Author field notes from November 5, 2014)

When the last of the soldiers left on July 31, 2015, Maré's various armed groups immediately re-established control of the community's streets. They have continued to occupy Maré's neighborhoods, as they had prior to the military's campaign. And municipal police, too, have returned to their violent operations and tactics. Indeed, in the last few years, Rio police have resorted to shooting into the community from helicopters, killing dozens, including innocent bystanders. Between 2016 and 2019, Rio police engaged in 129 operations that directly led to the deaths of 90 residents.[25] The violent status quo that has now persisted for several decades is a continuing source of frustration and trauma for Maré's residents. By focusing on citizens' lives and experiences and not the violence or

Figure 21. Spent shell casings discharged by soldiers and collected by a resident. Parque Rubens Vaz, Complexo da Maré, 2014.

crime that occurs around them, *Maré from the Inside* challenges the dominant and sensational narratives regarding policing and crime in Rio de Janeiro. It also offers a deeper appreciation of how residents have managed to survive amid these difficult circumstances.

CHAPTER 3
THE PORTRAITS OF *MARÉ FROM THE INSIDE* AND THEIR PRODUCTION

HENRIQUE GOMES

I was born and raised in Nova Holanda, one of Maré's 16 neighborhoods, and have lived there for most of my life. One of my passions growing up was music. I taught myself how to play the guitar and spent much of my youth playing with various groups and collectives throughout Maré. While this may seem like a small thing, anyone from Maré knows that such movement is fraught with danger. For as long as I can remember, different armed groups have operated in Maré, fighting for territory and control of illicit retail drug markets. Their presence has significantly limited the mobility of residents, who have internalized their rules and restrictions. My travels across those boundaries allowed me to develop a profound knowledge of Maré and its people. In turn, that understanding transformed me by giving me the tools to survive in a city in which every 23 minutes a young Black man from a favela is killed. It also led me to a profession and livelihood from which I have drawn meaning and purpose. On reflection, I have come to regard my long-term travels among Maré's neighborhoods and the expertise I acquired from those experiences as acts of resistance.

Nearly a decade ago, I began working with people from outside of Maré who came to conduct research. I offered to help them navigate the complex local social dynamics and to develop and implement plans to complete their various projects. Because most researchers knew next to nothing about Maré and its residents, I also sought to educate them by developing a long list of materials and resources about the Complexo. This process prompted me to reflect on situations that I had previously found natural and commonplace. For example, in preparation for the World Cup and Olympic Games, Rio's police significantly increased their presence and use of force throughout Maré. They began by apprehending many of the drug users and homeless people in areas immediately surrounding Maré. That action was followed by frequent incursions into the Complexo that targeted the drug trafficking factions. In June of 2013, a police sergeant was killed by traffickers during one such operation. In response, the Military Police proceeded to take over several areas of Maré, went from house to house searching for faction members, and eventually killed nine residents, several of whom had no known involvement with the factions. Within this context, I began to pay more attention to the international news coverage of Maré, which described it as a place filled with violence, poverty, and precarity. These hegemonic discourses implicitly accepted these police practices as necessary. For the first time in my life, I felt my reality was being directly affected by that narrative and came to agree with what some residents had been arguing for many years: "These claims must be disputed!"

Interiors of Maré

During the lead up to the World Cup in 2014, twenty residents from low-income and marginalized neighborhoods throughout South America came to Maré to participate in the São Paulo Artist Collective. The visitors stayed in Maré for one week, during which time I came to know and accompany Antonello Veneri, an Italian photographer, who was documenting their experience in Maré. At the end of the group's visit, he asked me if he could return to spend some more time. I readily agreed, offering him any guidance and support he needed.

When Antonello returned, he stayed for several months. We had many conversations during that time concerning how images of favelas are produced and how those communities are almost always portrayed as settings of violence and poverty. We also exchanged views concerning how advances in technology and the popularization of digital cameras and cell phones have led to a huge proliferation of favela images, created by residents as well as by outsiders.

Our dialogue prompted us to speak with several families living near my house in Nova Holanda to see if they were interested in helping us produce a photographic essay of family portraits. Even though the images grew out of my individual experiences in Maré, proposing to photograph my friends and neighbors inside their homes was a significant departure from my day-to-day life. Any reservations I had about the project, however, quickly dissipated during the first portrait experience. When we met Dona Penha, a woman in her 50s who worked in

Figure 22. Dona Jurema and her family. Nova Holanda, Complexo da Maré, 2013.

childcare, she remarked how she missed being photographed and observed that, when she was a child, their family would customarily gather to have their portraits taken during harvest festivals or religious fairs.

After visiting the second, third, and fourth families, we came to understand that we were developing a methodology centered on how the residents perceived the relationships among photography, family, and memory. We also began to understand that each of us had a role to play in this process. For my part, I used my knowledge of the community and its dense social networks and relations to reach out to families to ask them to participate. Antonello employed his significant artistic sensibilities and technical expertise. Meanwhile, the family members brought their memories, self-conceptions, and a desire to collaborate with us to portray how they imagined their community. Ultimately, we sought to employ photographs of the interiors of homes and of families to make visible what is not usually seen in the community. I illustrate this methodology and the experiences arising from these encounters by discussing four of the portraits that resulted from it.

Dona Jurema and Her Family (Fig. 22)

I have known Dona Jurema for many years. We worked together at a local NGO where she always treated everyone and everything, even the plants, with kindness and respect. During the afternoon we visited her house, we were discussing where to take the photo when we heard gunfire coming from the street. Dona Jurema, her six children, Antonello and I all ran onto the veranda for protection. Antonello and I immediately offered to take the photo another day, but she asked us to wait a little while before deciding. As we waited, Dona Jurema and her children spontaneously positioned themselves on the veranda in a natural, almost intuitive way. Antonello quickly set up the camera and took the photograph. At that exact moment, an enormous armored police truck (*caveirão*) appeared on the street in front of her house.

Life in Maré is marked by the need for residents to naturalize such moments of violence and fear. How do families, such as Dona Jurema's, alter their daily routines to deal with police operations, especially since they are so frequent? This question and the story behind this photo highlighted for Antonello and me the need to make visible these interior scenes so as to provoke a reevaluation of the responsibility of the whole of Brazilian society for the frequent imposition of violence in the daily lives of favela residents.

Dona Tânia and Carlos (Figs. 23, 24)

Tânia and Carlos' house is located in an area of Maré called McLaren, an old boat repair yard under a viaduct that has been converted into an informal settlement. Forty-four different families live in a very precarious and vulnerable situation there. These photographs address the issue of housing and other fundamental human rights denied these residents. In McLaren, the absence of these rights is visible in the improvised wooden and tent homes, the open sewers that flow directly into Guanabara Bay and various additional problems with sanitation and water distribution.

Tânia and Carlos had been living in their home for 12 years when we first photographed them. Upon entering, we immediately noticed a large number of sculptures and framed paintings. Tânia, who worked as a trash and recycling picker, said that her greatest joy

Figure 23. Dona Tânia Gonçalves and Luiz Carlos. Morro do Timbau, Complexo da Maré, 2014.

in life was to bring these found art objects back to her home. She indicated that she brought something home nearly every day. Tânia organized the room and the portrait to highlight some of the pieces she had collected over the years.

More than a year later, Antonello and I returned to present Tânia and Carlos with a large print of their portrait that we had used in an exhibition in Maré. Tânia was overjoyed with the photograph and placed it in her collection. Several months later, we returned again and found their home transformed. The couple had painted the walls a new color and the print we had given them was displayed prominently on one wall. We photographed them again.

Figure 24. Dona Tânia Gonçalves and Luiz Carlos. Morro do Timbau, Complexo da Maré, 2016.

The fact that Tânia and Carlos cared for their home so diligently, even in a situation of great vulnerability, did not surprise me as a favela resident. In fact, it reminded me of a phrase that my mother shared often when I was little, "We must take care of what is ours even if it is little." This adage suggests that caring for one's home organizes all the other functions of the day and it highlights favela residents' ever-present hopes and dreams.

Senhor Antônio (Fig. 25)

Senhor Antônio is representative of more than half of Maré's residents in that he is a migrant from the Northeast of Brazil, a region of significant social inequality that is also broadly stigmatized. My family is also a part of this history of migration. My parents came to Rio de Janeiro from the Northeastern state of Paraíba in search of employment

Figure 25. Senhor Antônio. Parque Maré, Complexo da Maré, 2013.

and the opportunities it afforded them and their children. Visiting Antônio and his wife, Dona Maria, brought back memories of the place where my parents were born and grew up because we were received with typical Northeastern food and stories about their life there before coming to Maré.

Antônio works in civil construction and is also an accordion player in a Forró band, a style of music popular in the Northeast. As I did with the guitar, he taught himself to play his instrument when he was a child. He then passed on his passion to all of his male children. I had come to know Antônio by frequently encountering him at shows in Maré. We immediately bonded over our love for music. Before taking his portrait, Antônio showed us an old photograph he had brought with him from the Northeast. It used a technique of mixing photography and painting/tinting that remained very popular until color film became widely available. Such framed photograph-paintings captured important events in the history of a family, such as weddings, baptisms and first communions.

Conclusion

The experience of producing these portraits demonstrated to Antonello and me the need to continue photographing families in a way that went beyond the traditional conceptions of a father (man), mother (woman), and children. We came to understand that the diversity of family types, such as those led by women, homoaffective families, multi-generational families, single mothers, and families without blood ties that become "family" through bonds of solidarity and survival, among many others, was something noteworthy that we needed to capture to tell the story of the community. And yet, we also noticed that the traditional idea of the nuclear family arose even when we asked a photographed family if they knew others who would like to participate. They always first proposed such family groups, because they thought that non-"traditional" families would not be welcome. We challenged that fear and narrative by including and photographing families that did not represent that stereotypical profile. This was, in part, a political decision resulting from the organic relationships on which *Maré from the Inside* was based. Honoring it became part of our working methodology.

After more than seven years photographing families in Maré, whenever I encounter one of our subjects on the street now, our conversation nearly always turns to the day we took their portrait. When that occurs, I gain a renewed sense of how this project has further strengthened the affective ties among Maré's residents. Those exchanges also remind me that this Exhibit shines a light on the richness and nuance of life in Maré, and for that, I find myself quite grateful.

CHAPTER 4
THE ARTISTIC POWER OF *MARÉ FROM THE INSIDE*

ANDREZA JORGE AND DESIRÉE POETS

How can images of a home and family speak to us about our own lives? That question guided our analysis of the four photographs discussed in this chapter. The portraits we examine pushed us to face our beliefs about gender, sexuality, race, class, parenthood, family and affection. As part of our creative process, we exchanged our perspectives concerning the photographs, which stemmed in part from our distinct lived experiences and relationships with the Exhibit and with Maré. Our views were also informed through active listening as we each considered the other's perceptions and, most importantly, allowed ourselves to be moved and inspired by them. In this way, for us, *Maré from the Inside* played its intended role of offering plural perspectives addressing the complexities of everyday life and of prompting surprising and yielding uncomfortable insights for those experiencing it. Indeed, the Exhibit generally, and the four photographs we consider here particularly, took each of us to new places intellectually and emotionally.

Maré from the Inside provokes such shifts in perspective, in part, through how it re-appropriates the hegemonic, Western-centric portrait of the traditional nuclear family[1] to represent instead a diverse favela community. The photographs, in portraying and highlighting the heterogeneity of individuals who reside in these private homes and spaces, promotes their acceptance "outside," in public spaces, as well. The portraits unsettle entrenched images and concepts about *being* in society, paving the way for decolonizing narratives.

Paulo and Matheus (Fig. 26)

The photo of Paulo and Matheus invites us to reflect on male affection and homoaffectivity,

Figure 26. Paulo Victor and Matheus Affonso. Nova Holanda, Complexo da Maré, 2018.

deconstructing the stigmas attached to such emotions and relationships. While homo affective and homosexual relationships have always existed, the Christian and Western-centric family model has long treated them as unnatural and immoral. This ethic has worked to make them invisible, while also often associating them with promiscuity and an absence of love and respect.

This photograph may unsettle us, encouraging us to think about this house's interior, in which the evident companionship between two men translates into an ambience of care. In doing so, it conjures up memories of our own families and the imaginaries we associate with them. Who cleans and cares for the house? Who cooks and sets the table? Who manages the family's finances? Such questions challenge prevailing and oppressive gender markers and encourage those experiencing them to contemplate, and perhaps even to forge, new realities: in which men are caring, affectionate and attentive; in which they love and demonstrate that love; in which they maintain a house jointly, turning it into their shared home.

The family life captured here contradicts the stereotypes concerning men in favela contexts, including, especially, the dominant association of masculinities and, in particular, Black masculinities, with aggressiveness. The representation of a homosexual couple in which one partner is Black only deepens this refutation. Finally, the objects in sight, the arrangement of the elements that comprise the photograph and the pose the young couple adopted, especially their assertive gaze, give us a sense of their personal tastes and preferences. Through this portrait, we can grasp how the subtleties of such stories lead to new imaginaries in which human diversity, in all its fullness, becomes non-negotiable.

Eliane, Herbet, Adriel Oliveira and Pipoca (Fig. 27)

This photograph immediately speaks to several oppressed social groups and peoples throughout the American continent who have survived despite centuries of European colonialism and imperialism. That survival has been anchored in ancestral knowledge, in forms of mutual assistance and self-help that we call "social technologies." Nuclear families, as an evocation of the production and individual logic and orientation of capitalist and neoliberal systems, follow a commercialized vision of child education. The old African proverb that "to educate a child, an entire village is needed" challenges that view. Favela communities have maintained that ancestral perspective. For example, the absence of government education policies to ensure the construction of adequate schools in these communities contributes to the fact that women who need to work to survive must delegate the care of their children to someone else. In most cases, children are entrusted to a grandmother or like figure. Put differently, in this common scenario in Maré and other favelas, another woman becomes responsible for the care of a family's children, repeating and naturalizing a cycle of care that becomes indistinguishable from what it means to be a woman, and especially a Black woman.

Having said this, we are not romanticizing stratified gender relations, nor the often precarious experience of Black women who need to work throughout their lives and who, even in their old age, remain essential to the reproduction of family life. We aim instead to propose an alternative perspective. This family scene, represented by a grandmother, grandchildren and a dog, evokes a utopia: That

Figure 27. Eliane Antunes, Herbet Oliveira dos Santos and Adriel Oliveira dos Santos. Dog: Pipoca. Nova Holanda, Complexo da Maré, 2014.

life, as the foundation of children's formation, can in fact be grounded in intergenerational love and passed on through rituals and stories shared by elders.

Kelly and Gael (Fig. 28)

This portrait evokes a mother's strength and warmth. Facing the camera, Kelly places a protective arm over Gael, her young son, who cuddles up to her in obvious comfort but nonetheless seems wary of the camera. Kelly leaves much of the couch's space to Gael, who is in the center of the photograph, literally making space for him. But she is not made smaller by that generous act: her body language is wide and open, her legs graciously crossed to the side. She is beautiful. Against common flawed depictions of mothers as passive and

Figure 28. Kelly Santos and Gael Aguiar. Nova Holanda, Complexo da Maré, 2018.

subordinate in the traditional, heteronormative family structure, this portrait communicates female dignity, power and agency. And against the reductive representation of working-class neighborhoods such as favelas as places of squalor, the soft light and thoughtful organization and positioning of the furniture bespeak instead an intentional and affirming aesthetic.

Kelly's elegant posture reminds onlookers of matriarchal traditions in many non-Western cultures that heteropatriarchal Eurocentrism has sought to replace.[2] Maroons, or *quilombos*, in Brazil, which are communities of African and slave ancestry, are regularly led by women, for example.[3] In addition, women have always played a strong role in working-class communities. In an environment of precarity

Figure 29. Vera Marcelino. Parque Maré, Complexo da Maré, 2013.

and government neglect, which has long characterized life in Rio's favelas, women have routinely assumed positions of leadership *and* care. Motherhood and femininity here are not debilitating, but instead a source and expression of power, including the capacity to care not just for oneself, but also for the past, present and future of a family and community.

Vera (Fig. 29)

The process through which drug use has come to be treated as a crime in Brazil rather than a public health concern, (re-)produces marginalization by normalizing state neglect and discrimination against drug users, especially when they are of Black and working-class backgrounds. Crack cocaine has been the most recent addition to this landscape in Rio, arriving in the city in the early 2000s. Its use and sale find socio-spatial expression in stigmatized territories called "*cracolândia*" (in English "crackland").[4]

The "crack scene" in Maré, depicted in this photograph, was also an immediate result of the Police Pacification Units (see Chapter 2), which pushed people who use that drug and struggle with homelessness out of other communities where UPPs were installed. That is, the use and sale of drugs in a city, including in Rio, are not just the result of individual decisions. They are also tied to public policy and structural conditions.

In this photograph, "home," "family" and "belonging" take on forms and meaning beyond the physical structure of a house or apartment. Meaningful human connections are also built in seemingly ephemeral spatial arrangements. We find elements commonly associated with a *living* room: people are sitting with one another on couches by a coffee table, on which notebooks full of scribbles and an unfinished card game lie. Vera, facing the camera, sits in a relaxed posture with her legs crossed, smoking a cigarette. Like most of us when we are at home, she has taken one shoe off, letting her foot rest. She is home. Nonetheless, the photograph does not romanticize this "scene." It also unsettles us, laying bare the structural inequalities that shape it as it conveys the prejudice and stigma that the people in it experience, who chose, at the last minute, to hide their faces, opening up several possible interpretations of that act. In this way, the photograph embodies the contradictions and disjunctions of life in such a "scene."

Conclusion

The portraits discussed here depict the favela as a plural space in which the diversity of home interiors reflects a diversity of people, family constellations and emotional ties. In doing so, they challenge any reduction of them to a space "of exception"––of squalor, abjection, disconnection, violence and criminality––in which both state repression and neglect are normalized. Maré emerges, instead, in its full human complexity, as a community in which everyday life goes on in the face of precarity, stigmatization and marginalization.

CHAPTER 5
FAMILY CONSTELLATIONS AND AFFECTIVE BONDS IN *MARÉ FROM THE INSIDE*

MOLLY F. TODD

This chapter arose from a series of conversations between a long-time Maré resident, Andreza Jorge, and me. I reflect here on those discussions as a way to consider larger questions about favela family life and identity in relation to globalized social structures of systemic discrimination. As a Ph.D. student in the U.S. who resides in Blacksburg, Virginia, I come to *Maré from the Inside* as an American citizen who has not yet been to Brazil. From this position, I consider our dialogue in light of three different portraits. I contend that while the Exhibit reflects unique and specific stories of place, it simultaneously speaks to a diverse set of family constellations, love and affective bonds. The heterogeneity of life in Maré represented in these photographs not only pushes back against a singular idea of family, but also challenges the static subjectivities assigned to favela residents by the wider Brazilian society and in other nations, as both recipients and originators of violence. Relatedly, the engagement with *Maré from the Inside* that I offer here, as an outsider, illustrates the Exhibit's potential to break with constructions of favela communities as radical Others to whom U.S. Americans cannot relate. It does so by pointing to a shared human experience as well as to the systems of oppression that cross the North and South of the Americas without losing sight of local context and specificities.

I begin by analyzing Jorge's portrait and story in relation to systemic discrimination. I then reflect on the diverse family and gender relations in Maré, turning to two additional photographs included in the Exhibit. I conclude by contending that art and culture can open our imaginations by challenging stereotypes and homogenous visions of favela domestic and family life.

Figure 30. Andreza Jorge and Alice Odara, Nova Holanda, Complexo da Maré, 2016.

Andreza and Alice (Fig. 30)

The photograph above illustrates one of the many stories of family life in Maré. Jorge is seated, breastfeeding her daughter in the portrait. She at once evidences comfort, strength and love for her daughter. While this photograph brings viewers into just a single room, it simultaneously evokes a more universal story of family, belonging and home. This image of a mother's love and her quiet dignity directly challenges stereotypes of favelas as places of crime, despair and broken lives.

These prevailing understandings, structured through racist, patriarchal and heteronormative systems of discrimination, produce many injustices. For example, Black women in Brazil, and in the Americas more broadly, disproportionately experience police violence in comparison to other women.[1] Indeed, Jorge commented during our conversations that her very existence— being Black, Latin American, Brazilian and a

Figure 31. Sofia Felicidade and Dona Maria. Parque Maré, Complexo da Maré, 2016.

favelada—are identities that place her in the dominant Western imaginary as "outsider," or Other. The fact that Maré is a favela located in the Global South too often relegates those who live there to the margins of society. Jorge's story illustrates that such structural conditions do not simply determine the lives of favela residents, however. It is in this tension, between the conditions of state violence and neglect on the one hand, and the diversity and dignity of their lives on the other, that these individuals act to mobilize their community and to express their agential capacities, including through works of art, such as *Maré from the Inside*.

The cultural and artistic production that arises from favelas, including the photographs and films that comprise this Exhibit, offers a different perspective of these communities, one which provides a more nuanced and layered reflection of life than that depicted in conventional or hegemonic understandings.[2]

I interpret Jorge's determined and unwavering gaze as representing not only a journey of struggle, but also one of love and fulfillment.

Jorge reflected on her life experiences to date during our conversations. After growing up in Maré, she married and moved outside her community of origin, although still within the larger city of Rio. Soon after her daughter, Alice Odara, was born, Jorge's marriage ended. As she coped with raising a newborn and her professional obligations alone, she was drawn back to her family in Maré. Jorge returned home to the welcoming and supportive embrace of her mother and brother. Their affective bonds were maintained despite the fact that she had left. Her return suggests that favelas are not simply places of poverty and lawlessness from which to "escape," but rather communities to which individuals may turn to raise and nurture their own families. Jorge's experience highlights the fact that favela women routinely build families and careers within their communities with the help of family and friends.

Sofia and Dona Maria, Nelson with Dog (Figs. 31, 32)

Two additional photographs suggest that favela family constellations, like countless others across the world, cannot be captured in a single story or idea. For example, when Jorge spent time at her brother's house, she eventually became acquainted with one of his friends, Henrique Gomes. They came to know each other and formed an enduring bond that eventually led to their marriage. Their ties arose not only through their love for one another, but also via what became a shared love for Alice. Gomes' embrace of fatherhood reflects a non-biological family constellation that not only pushes against the stereotype of the absent Black father, but also connects Exhibit viewers to the many ways in which families form and find love all over the world.

These two portraits express additional types of family units and suggest that affective bonds can develop in many different forms. For example, the photo on the left shows the love between a grandmother and granddaughter. Dona Maria's smile exudes joy while her granddaughter Sofia's embrace suggests security, comfort and trust. This photograph of intergenerational affection demonstrates the ways in which family constellations in Maré contest the overrepresentation or spectacle of insecurity and fear in the favelas.[3] It also challenges their reduction to spaces of immorality and "broken families," pointing instead to how they are spaces in which extended family members are in close relationship with one another. Moreover, the image of the little girl with her grandmother in a room ornamented with flowers and whimsical colors evokes a future with many potential paths and horizons. Their

Figure 32. Nelson Teixeira with dog. Parque Maré, Complexo da Maré, 2016.

embrace suggests mutual loving support, while the butterflies on the mirror above the pair can be read as symbols of hope, endurance and freedom. Put differently, Maré, like any human community, offers its residents the promise of hope and opportunities to pursue their dreams. The prospect of thriving, and not simply just surviving, exists in Maré.

Finally, the portrait of the man with his dog demonstrates that affective bonds are not only formed between humans. Nelson holds his small dog close to his heart, and his facial expression resonates with a sense of pride that does not read as traditionally masculine. Rather, there is gentleness in this scene, underscored by the teal-colored walls and the dim lighting circling what appears to be a memorial. This scene reminds us that masculinity can also be sensitive and calls into question the dominant stereotypic image of all favela men as violent or criminal. More broadly, it challenges systems of patriarchy that reflect static conceptions of gender. This photograph, alongside others in the Exhibit, demonstrates that the many different individuals in Maré together comprise a rich tapestry of family constellations, a variety that in fact may be found in communities all over the world.

    The depictions of family life in *Maré from the Inside* not only challenge a single story or idea of family, but also questions the larger narrative within Brazilian society and globally that favelas are places of emptiness and fragmented family structures and community life. The portraits and narratives of this Exhibit instead capture and evoke a heterogeneous community. They inspire their viewers to recall the diversity and complexity of their own families. These photographs also demand that those contemplating them consider how their own class, race and gender identity may affect how they envision family and the possible trajectories their own lives could take, and why. The Exhibit facilitates a multi-faceted and multi-layered imaginative encounter with Maré that does not yield a simple or single story of family, place, identity or community. Instead, the many elements of *Maré from the Inside* open viewers to the diverse possibilities of love, family and hope.

CHAPTER 6
TRUTH-TELLING, MEANING MAKING, AND IMAGINING FRESH POSSIBILITIES

MAX O. STEPHENSON JR.

This volume and its associated Exhibit challenge those individuals who have accepted a view of favelas as uniformly troubled, poor and dangerous. *Maré from the Inside* asks such people to reconsider their views of favelas and favela life, and thereby to imagine and to explore a new order of possibilities that honor the dignity and diverse lived reality of the individuals and families who call these communities home. The Exhibit and this book can be understood to build on Lícia do Prado Valladares' contention that historical, social and academic representations of these communities have systematically misled many into considering them as alike in three overarching ways:

> The first is that of specificity: the favela is a different place from the rest of the city. The second is that the favela is the urban locus of poverty. The third is that of unity: unity between favelas, unity within the favela.[1]

That is, scholars and citizens alike have been willing to treat these neighborhoods and populations stereotypically by adopting perspectives and descriptions that obscure their vibrancy, vitality and heterogeneity. Analysts have for too long portrayed favelas as zones of exception, rather than as immensely complex and integral parts of the society of which their populations are a part. As Valladares has suggested, this willingness to subject these communities to a process of reductive categorization has too often also occurred on the part of the Brazilian government.[2] These long-lived realities raise the question of what might be necessary both to challenge these dominant oppressive frames and for those living outside these communities to adopt new perspectives predicated instead

Figure 33. Two women during a Brazil World Cup game. Nova Holanda, Complexo da Maré, 2014.

on the generative reality of everyday life in these neighborhoods. This Exhibit aims to further just such a potential.

Shifting epistemic claims is never a straightforward matter of presenting new or contrary information and magically attaining social change. Instead, sense-making frames are notoriously sticky. In fact, shifts in these often unconsciously held values and norms can only occur by means of a reimagining of the phenomenon whose definition or value is in question. The poet Gregory Orr remarked some years ago, while treating the power of lyric poetry as an entrée to unimagined possibilities, that one must first acknowledge and imagine the embodied self before one can employ poetry to help construct order in a disorderly world. He reminded his readers that human beings crave order, and that condition is typically secured via the construction and acceptance of a broadly shared story or narrative:

And this unbearableness of disorder brings us to a second awareness: that each of us needs a sense of order, a sense that some patterns or enduring principles are at work in our lives. Though the tolerance for disorder varies from individual to individual, no one can live in a world of complete randomness. … To be human is to have a deep craving for order.[3]

Importantly, and as Orr emphasized, individuals exercise their imaginations to make sense of the world they encounter. As they cross the thresholds of the entries to their homes with their known boundaries and move into the unpredictably chaotic world beyond, people rely on stories to help them make sense of the realities they encounter. But they cannot do so unless they first acknowledge the disorder they confront, or as Orr wrote: "It is the initial act of surrendering to disorder that permits the ordering powers of the imagination to assert themselves."[4]

The lesson of this insight, as one ponders the photographs and videos that comprise this Exhibit, is that its renderings of the daily lives of those who live in Maré evoke a reality that demands a shift in the binary and banal stereotypes of Othering that have for so long placed this population apart in the public imagination. Here instead are photographs of individuals celebrating their favorite soccer team (see fig. 33); children, as all children are wont to do, finding a way to make a happenstance, a fallen tree, a space for all sorts of play-filled possibilities (see fig. 34); and of family members in their homes dining, watching television or conversing. Here too, are images of residents gathering with curiosity and fear to witness the imposition of the broader society's militaristic power in their midst (see fig. 35). And here as well is a photograph of a woman caring for her neighbor's child so that the latter may work; what Andreza Jorge and Desirée Poets elsewhere in this volume call a "social technology" of communal self-help and mutual assistance (see fig. 36). This Exhibit and its powerful images press observers to acknowledge the story that too many have imposed on this population and to imagine the dissolution and reconstruction or reordering of that vision.

In short, despite the exigencies imposed by the suppression of a broader society too often content to Other these citizens and to place them into false and reductive binary categories, these images of everyday life in this Rio neighborhood paint a tableau of heterogeneity, courage, frailty, fear, stubbornness and courage. They constitute an homage to a human community more alike than unalike any other one might profile. In so doing, and as Marcuse has argued more broadly of the possibility implicit in all art, *Maré from the Inside* both reveals the procreative energy of the community it

Figure 34. Children playing on a fallen tree after a storm. Nova Holanda, Complexo da Maré, 2016.

Figure 35. Residents watch the actions of the Brazilian Armed Forces during the Occupation. Parque Rubens Vaz, Complexo da Maré, 2014.

captures and contests the dominant story on offer concerning its residents:

> … art is inevitably part of that which is and only as part of that which is does it speak against that which is. This contradiction is preserved and resolved (aufgehoben) in the aesthetic form which gives the familiar content and the familiar experience the power of estrangement—and which leads to the emergence of a new consciousness and a new perception.[5]

Simply, this Exhibit demands a reimagining of previously adopted unjust and inaccurate renderings of this community's people and lives. These photographs and short films prompt those who experience them to enter Orr's space of disorder and dissolution and reconsider their received views and values and construct different ones.

While no art alone can guarantee the full rendering of this possibility—of what Paulo Freire has labeled conscientization—for all who contemplate it, the power of *Maré from the Inside* inheres in its embrace of the quotidian, the everyday, and the powerful challenge that focus raises for prevailing social stereotypes and narrative.[6] That contestation is surely Marcusian in its reach, possible power, and dynamic. It is likewise a potent reminder of the importance of taking the daily lives of individuals and their shared realities seriously in all efforts to describe their communities. The French philosopher Michel de Certeau captured the enormous significance of observing what he dubbed *The Practice of Everyday Life* in order to glean the daily rhythms of communities and to detect the ways in which their residents were addressing injustice and oppression.[7] Andrew Blauvelt captured the import of Certeau's insights in an essay concerning the role of design in everyday life:

> Certeau's investigations into the realm of routine practices, or the "arts of doing" such as walking, talking, reading, dwelling, and cooking, were guided by his belief that despite repressive aspects of modern society, there exists an element of creative resistance to these structures enacted by ordinary people … de Certeau outline[d] an important critical distinction between strategies and tactics in this battle of repression and expression. According to him, strategies are used by those within organizational power structures, whether small or large, such as the state or municipality, the corporation or the proprietor, a scientific enterprise or the scientist. … Tactics, on the other hand, are employed by those who are subjugated. By their very nature tactics are defensive and opportunistic, used in more limited ways and seized momentarily within spaces, both physical and psychological, produced and governed by more powerful strategic relations.[8]

The photographs and videos that comprise this Exhibit offer a lens into a society whose inherent mosaic-like complexity and whose very lived realities, in de Certeau's terms, constitute not merely a defensive reaction to the stereotypes pressed upon its population, but a generative evocation of a community of spirit, diversity, vibrancy and resilience. This Exhibit's images capture a society and its residents going about their lives, and in so doing they encourage a reimagining of that population and of the character of their community as well. As Marcuse might suggest, the art on view here questions false binaries, narratives, and imaginaries, instead evoking a population of heterogeneity of purpose and possibility.

In a very real sense, *Maré from the Inside* asks its viewers to confront reality through the faculty of their imagination and to begin the process of improvising—an integral part of imagining—a new narrative

Figure 36. A woman takes care of her neighbor's daughter. Many residents rely on this form of mutual support in their daily lives.

that comports both to the truth of what they have encountered and to the promise that it represents. In that sense, this Exhibit asks that its observers make meaning alongside those to whose lives they are permitted partial entry and to reconsider and re-found their assumptions of those residents as they do so. The art on view here promises the potential to open pathways to new meanings and to changed conditions and thereby to fresh possibilities to realize social justice.

CONCLUSION:
ON THE STRUGGLE FOR FREEDOM AND DIGNITY

MAX O. STEPHENSON JR.

Apart from emphasizing throughout the vibrancy and hope present in Maré, this volume, and the Exhibit it accompanies, evidence at least three principal themes, each of which is rooted deeply in the human condition and its capacity for, or lack of, imagination. First, as described briefly below and treated more fully in chapter 1, Rio's favelas were originally settled disproportionately by emancipated former slaves. That fact has come with continuing and bitter social, economic and political costs related to ongoing discrimination against residents of those communities, on the basis of their skin color and social class.

Second, while slavery and its accompanying dehumanization of people of color was practiced in Brazil for more than 350 years, the opprobrium and oppression that fact's long shadow has cast on the ancestors of such citizens in that nation has been exacerbated in recent decades by the quickening pace of globalization and the abiding anxiety those forces have created. Individuals feeling deeply anxious about their social and economic standing have too often turned to Othering and scapegoating the nation's poor and the residents of its favelas, particularly, to assuage those concerns. The costs of this turn, as highlighted in chapter 2, have often been high.

Third, if these historical currents together constitute a double-barreled assault on democratic possibility and equality for favela citizens, this Exhibit demonstrates that this community's population has refused to concede to the social tyranny of the failure of imagination they represent. Rather, those residents have continued to go about their lives, to raise and educate their children and to pursue their livelihoods, even as they have persistently argued that they be treated by their nation's governments and other citizens with the same standing and respect accorded other Brazilians. Chapters 4-6 illustrated this point repeatedly. I point particularly here, by way of example, to Henrique Gomes' description in chapter 3 of Dona Tânia Goncalves and Luiz Carlos, who carefully decorated their home with art even as the circumstances in which they lived were extremely difficult, by any measure.

Ultimately, *Maré from the Inside* tells a story of quiet dignity and profound humanity. This community's residents seek no more, and certainly no less, than their rights to be accorded freedom and equality. It remains to be seen whether their continuing efforts and those of the many others who support their claims, will prove sufficient to overcome the inertia of anxiety and hate predicated on fear of difference. One thing does seem certain: Maré's residents' collective will to survive and to be accorded the place their humanity bespeaks is indomitable and will endure. In many respects, this Exhibit and text are testimony to that fact, even as they are testament as well to the imagination and moral courage of the population they depict.

An Emancipated Population?

Chapter 1 of this volume, which sketched the history of Rio's favelas, made clear that they were initially settled principally by freed slaves in the early 1890s soon after the formal ending of slavery in Brazil in 1888. Building on more than three and a half centuries of dehumanization, favelas and their residents came to be considered communities of vice, iniquity and laziness by much of Brazilian society. This set of morally empty and brazenly cruel social attitudes set in train much of the continuing oppression and racist discrimination that Maré's citizens have continued to encounter since their ancestors' emancipation. While hardly the product of Brazilian society alone, as this sort of behavior is endemic to humankind and has occurred across all of human history, the enduring character of the negative attitudes originally conceived to "justify" enslavement nonetheless has portended a sharp circumscription of the specific moral responsibilities that Brazil's political and economic elite has since felt obliged to acknowledge for this population.

While modern day conceptions of democracy, human rights and moral duty demand an in-principle absolute willingness to accord all persons dignity and political equality, many Brazilians have often been content instead to deny that standing to favela residents on the basis of an Othering rooted ultimately in a willingness to separate "us" from "them" on grounds of perceived "differences" that hearken to the days of slavery. The evocative portraits and photographs of this Exhibit reveal the hollowness of that disposition and highlight thereby its ethical bankruptcy. The Polish sociologist Zygmunt Bauman has captured this point elegantly:

> Being moral means, in the nutshell, knowing the difference between good and evil and where to draw a line between them—as well as being able to tell one from another when you watch them in action or contemplate enacting them. By extension it also means recognizing one's own … [r]esponsibility for promoting good and resisting evil. … To put the matter bluntly: what is wholly and unconditionally alien to the quality of "being moral," and what militates against it, is the tendency to halt and renounce moral responsibility for others at the border drawn between "us" and "them."[1]

Maré from the Inside calls on Brazilian society writ large to recognize and acknowledge the rights of an important portion of its population. It de facto broadens and deepens that appeal by demanding that all of humanity, i.e., all who encounter its photographs, films and portraits, irrespective of their provenance, do the same.

An Era of Globalized Marketization, Widespread Anxiety and Scapegoating

Another source of continuing discrimination against favela residents is the widespread embrace of neoliberalism as public philosophy amidst the quickening pace of economic and social globalization in recent decades. Brazil has adopted a neoliberal conception of the state, which leaves individuals deeply vulnerable and increasingly alone to confront the vagaries of the marketplace. Perversely, this situation has meant that residents of favelas have been hit doubly hard by globalization and especially in the period leading up to the 2014 and 2016 sports mega-events, during which Rio's government adopted an urban entrepreneurial governance model.[2] The city's promotion of urban renewal projects, such as Porto Maravilha in the port area, and investments in infrastructure, including in transport and sanitation, through public-private partnerships deepened Rio's existing socio-spatial inequalities by leading to gentrification and the further concentration of services in the city's privileged neighborhoods. The Police Pacification Units (UPPs), which combined physical force and pedagogical programs, were central to this process that overall aimed to 'secure' the city for foreign investments and to reshape favela residents' behavior by disciplining them into neoliberal subjects.[3] The militarization described in chapter 2 that has disproportionately targeted Rio's favela residents can therefore also be described as a mechanism to regulate the poor so as to support neoliberal urbanization.[4]

More broadly, neoliberalism has also created anxiety in the broader Brazilian population to the extent that increased competition has dampened wages and negatively affected employment rates, a scenario aggravated by the economic recessions Brazil has faced since its staging of the two sports mega-events noted above. The latter trend has encouraged the continued scapegoating and Othering of favela residents that, as an organizing principle of social relations in Brazil, serves as a misguided mechanism for other citizens to cope with the social and economic challenges they have confronted. Bauman has also neatly captured this parlous state of insecurity:

> The widespread sense of existential insecurity is a hard fact: a genuine bane of our society that prides itself, through the lips of its political leaders, on the progressive deregulation of labour markets, and flexibilization of work, and thus, as a result is notorious for propagating a growing fragility of social positions and instability of socially recognized identities—as well as for unstoppable expansion of the ranks of the precariat.[5]

Dignity and Freedom Despite Enduring Adversity

Maré's residents have never accepted their demeaned and diminished social and political status, despite continuing social oppression and scapegoating wrought by long-term Othering predicated on perceived difference and fears, as well as bearing the brunt of a national securitization effort ahead of Rio hosting the Olympics and World Cup earlier in the past decade. They have instead continued to organize efforts to ensure service provision and advocacy on behalf of the community's population and to petition the nation's governments to offer the support to which they are legally entitled, but which they too often do not receive. That is, Maré's residents have not only continued actively to protest the injustices they confront, but also individually and collectively have worked generatively to develop efforts to address many concerns in their community themselves. In this, they have not only exercised their individual and collective political agency, but also demanded its recognition by their fellow citizens. Those initiatives are simultaneously ensuring services of various sorts to the community.

In all of these efforts, and as the dignity manifest in so many of the photographs and portraits of this Exhibit illustrates, this population has never lost hope, nor a sense of purpose. As Spinoza noted in his *Ethics*: "Emotion, which is suffering ceases to be suffering as soon as we form a clear and precise picture of it."[6] One way that Maré's citizens have developed a shared purpose, and therefore meaning, has been in confronting daily discrimination and injustice. This Exhibit demonstrates that life's meaning arises with purpose. Even amidst extraordinary and long-lived injustice, human beings can find reasons for living and demanding that others acknowledge and account for their existence. Victor Frankl has recounted speaking to his fellow concentration camp prisoners of their shared suffering at an especially low moment during their time at Auschwitz:

> I asked [those] who listened to me attentively in the darkness of the hut to face up to the seriousness of our position. They must not lose hope, but should keep their courage in the certainty that the hopelessness of our struggle did not detract from its meaning or dignity and its meaning.[7]

I turn to Frankl's work here not to draw a comparison between those camps and favelas, but to stress instead the deeper point of how, in contexts of precarity and violence, people have found ways of making meaning and affirming life. Indeed, *Maré from the Inside* highlights the many ways that the community's residents have engaged in just this process amidst the continuing social oppression and difficult economic circumstances that many of its residents have long confronted.

As this Exhibit suggests repeatedly, the residents of Maré may not soon overcome the inhumanity too often visited on them as a result of their skin color, economic status or residence location, but that fact has nothing whatever to do with their innate humanity or the significance or meaning of their struggle to achieve widespread recognition of their rights and rightful freedom. No person can deny another human being that purpose, and no such purpose could be more important and fulsome, nor more inspiring than that of the favela residents profiled here. I hope those reading this volume and encountering this Exhibit gain a hint of this nearly unfathomable reality, innate to both human freedom and imagination.

AFTERWORD

We have sought to make this book as accessible to as wide a readership as possible. In particular, there are three distinct audiences to which this volume and its accompanying Exhibit speak. First, for researchers and students of favelas and marginalized communities, more broadly, the methodology we have developed to produce this work offers an avenue of analysis and engagement that challenges existing hierarchies within the academy, which elevate specialized scholarly knowledge production above community-based dialogue and writing for a broader audience. At every step, we have dedicated ourselves to horizontality, accountability and self-reflexivity rather than to a set of predetermined outputs or box-ticking exercises. Such a form of collaboration has not come without conflict and disagreement, but we have found dialogue around these differences to offer numerous opportunities to learn from one another. Our hope is that scholars, activists and artists will replicate and further elaborate on this methodology in other contexts.

The second audience we have sought to address are those learning about Rio's favelas for the first time and with perhaps only limited knowledge of Brazil and its social and political relations. Through *Maré from the Inside*'s photographs and videos as well as this book's short and accessible chapters, we have sought to expand understanding of these communities by, first, appreciating their vibrancy and diversity and, second, highlighting how hegemonic media narratives have skewed and distorted popular understandings of these communities and encouraged and justified excessively punitive public policy in so doing. Our hope is that citizens of the United States and other countries in the Global North will recognize how similarly biased frames have been applied to marginalized communities within their own societies.

The third audience we have had in mind while writing this book are the residents of Maré. We have translated each chapter into Portuguese for a separate volume so that the families that participated in the project and anyone else interested in Maré can read and appreciate its arguments. We hope that the perspective on view here and the visibility it offers of the lived experiences of this community's residents will constitute a source of pride and validation for them. The history and analysis chapters are also intended to complement and further encourage community-building projects and ongoing discussions of collective memory among Maré's citizens. Relatedly, we hope that this book can serve to support residents' struggles for structural change in Rio and Brazil, and that it stands as recognition for how political agency and artistic production in Maré open up more just horizons not only in Brazil but also in other parts of the world.

In the coming years, *Maré from the Inside* will continue to travel to academic institutions and other spaces in the United States and Europe so as to share the vibrancy of the community with as many audiences as possible. We plan to conclude the global tour of *Maré from the Inside* by presenting the Exhibit in one of several public spaces within the Complexo. Thereafter, we will give the portraits to the various families that participated in the project and find a permanent home for the remainder in a local arts institution.

On a more personal note, the collaborators wish to express how transformative this project has been for them. In separate but related ways, we have been forced to question many of our assumptions regarding academic research, engagement with the public and the role of arts in community change. Moreover, after nearly a decade of collaboration and numerous interactions with audiences throughout the United States, we have become only further convinced of the necessity of this project and its interrelated objectives of challenging stigmatizing and racist narratives concerning favelas and their inhabitants, decolonizing academia by creating more horizontal relationships between these communities in Rio and academic institutions in the Global North, and developing a new set of cultural strategies that make space for marginalized communities in the Brazilian national body politic.

ENDNOTES

INTRODUCTION

1. Jesus, Diego (Director). "Ocupação" ["Occupation"] [video]. Escola de Cinema Olhares da Maré, 2014. https://www.youtube.com/watch?v=kZ9quSHhTeo

2. Kirschenbaum, Jill (Senior Producer). "Girl's Life: Maria Luiza Santos, 14, Rio de Janeiro" [video]. *The Wall Street Journal*, November 25, 2015. https://www.wsj.com/video/girl-life-maria-luiza-santos-15-rio-de-janeiro/3AE8DA1F-3134-4FBA-9B9E-953DFEC6D168.html

3. Guardian Music. "Metanóia Church: Where Heavy Metal is a Form of Worship" [video]. YouTube. January 22, 2016. https://www.youtube.com/watch?v=_HS7MDPsdu8&feature=emb_logo

CHAPTER 1

1. Instituto Pereira Passos. (2018). *Limite de Favelas e Urbanização [Favela Boundaries and Urbanization]* [Data File]. Retrieved from https://www.data.rio/datasets/limites-de-favelas-e-urbanização

2. Perlman, Janice E. *Favela: Four Decades of Living on the Edge in Rio de Janeiro*. Oxford, UK: Oxford University Press, 2010, p. 25.

3. Chalhoub, Sidney. *Cidade Febril: Cortiços e Epidemias Na Corte Imperial [Fever City: Cortiços and Epidemics at the Imperial Court]*. Rio de Janeiro: Companhia das Letras, 1996, pp. 15–20; Fischer, Brodwyn. *A Poverty of Rights: Citizenship and Inequality in Twentieth-Century Rio de Janeiro*. Stanford, CA: Stanford University Press, 2008, p. 33; Vaz, Lillian Fessler. *História Dos Bairros Da Maré: Espaço, Tempo e Vida Cotidiana No Complexo Da Maré [A History of the Neighorhoods of Maré: Space, Time and Everyday Life]*. Rio de Janeiro: Federal University of Rio de Janeiro, 1994, p. 59.

4. Voyages Database. *Voyages: The Trans-Atlantic Slave Trade Database*. 2016. https://www.slavevoyages.org

5. Fischer, 2008, pp. 223–224.

6. Penglase, Benjamin. *Living with Insecurity in a Brazilian Favela: Urban Violence and Daily Life*. New Brunswick, NJ: Rutgers University Press, 2014.

7   Carvalho, Bruno. *Porous City: A Cultural History of Rio de Janeiro*. Liverpool, UK: Liverpool University Press, 2013.

8   Santos, Carlos Ferreira dos. *O Morro Do Timbau* [*Timbau Hill*]. Niterói, BR: Federal Fluminense University, 1983.

9   Santo, Andréia Martins de Oliveira, Dalcio Marinho Gonçalves, and Eliana Sousa Silva. "Contextualizando a Maré" ["Contextualizing Maré"]. In *Vivências Educativas Na Maré: Desafios e Possibilidades* [*Educational Experiences in Maré: Challenges and possibilities*], edited by Andréia Martins de Oliveira Santo and Eliana Sousa Silva. Rio de Janeiro: Redes da Maré, 19–34, 2013, p. 21; Santos, 1983, p. 44.

10 Ribeiro da Silva, Claudia Rose. *Maré: A Invenção de Um Bairro* [*Maré: The invention of a neighborhood*]. Rio de Janeiro: Fundação Getúlio Vargas, 2006.

11 Vaz, 1994, p. 158.

12 Vaz, 1994, p. 167.

13 "Um Presidente Solitário" ["A Solitary President"] *União Da Maré*, *1*(2), 3, 1980.

14 Ribeiro da Silva, 2006, p. 103.

15 Vieira, Antônio Carlos Pinto. *Histórico Da Maré* [*History of Maré*]. Rio de Janeiro: CEASM, 1998, p. 72.

16 Jones, Claire. "História Do 'Projeto Rio' Na Maré Parte 1: O Canto Da Sereia" ["History of 'Projeto Rio in Maré Part 1: The Song of the Mermaid"] *Rio on Watch*. July 16, 2017. https://rioonwatch.org.br/?p=26789

17 Jones, Claire. "História Do 'Projeto Rio' Na Maré Parte 2: Aliados Juntem-Se à Luta" ["History of 'Projeto Rio in Maré Part 2: Allies, join the struggle"]. *Rio on Watch*. September 5, 2017. https://rioonwatch.org.br/?p=26952

18 Jones, Claire. "História Do 'Projeto Rio' Na Maré Parte 3: Desagregação Do Governo" ["History of 'Projeto Rio in Maré Part 3: The Dismantling of the Government"]. *Rio on Watch*. September 20, 2017. https://rioonwatch.org.br/?p=2818

CHAPTER 2

1   Holloway, Thomas. H. *Policing Rio de Janeiro: Repression and Resistance in a 19th-Century City*. Stanford, CA: Stanford University Press, 1993.

2   Penglase, Benjamin. "The Bastard Child of the Dictatorship." *Luso-Brazilian Review*, *45*(1), 118–145, 2008, p. 130.

3   Perlman, Janice E. *The Myth of Marginality: Urban Poverty and Politics in Rio de Janeiro*. Berkeley, CA: University of California Press, 1976, pp. 258–260.

4   Franco, Marielle. "UPP – A redução da favela a três letras: Uma análise da política de segurança pública do Estado do Rio de Janeiro" ["UPP – The Reduction of the Favela to Three Letters: An Analysis of Rio de Janeiro's State Public Security Policy"]. Master's Thesis: Universidade Federal Fluminense, 2014. https://app.uff.br/riuff/handle/1/2166; Leeds, Elizabeth. "Cocaine and Parallel Polities in the Brazilian Urban Periphery: Constraints on Local-Level Democratization." *Latin American Research Review*, *31*(3), 1996, p. 66.

5   Misse, Michel. *Malandros, Marginais e Vagabundos & a acumulação social da violência no Rio de Janeiro*. Doctoral Dissertation: Instituto Universitário de Pesquisas do Rio de Janeiro, 1999. http://www.uece.br/labvida/dmdocuments/malandros_marginais_e_vagabundos_michel_misse.pdf

6   Souza e Silva, Jailson de, Fernando Lannes Fernandes, and Raquel Willadino Braga. "Grupos Criminosos Armados Com Domínio de Território" ["Armed Criminal Groups with Control over Territory"]. In *Segurança, tráfico e milícia no Rio de Janeiro* [*Security, trafficking and militia in Rio de Janeiro*], edited by Justiça Global. Rio de Janeiro: Justiça Global, 16–24, 2008.

7   Amorim, Carlos. *Comando Vermelho, A História Secreta Do Crime Organizado* [*Comando Vermelho: The Secret History of Organized Crime*]. Rio de Janeiro: Record, 1993.

8   Andreoni, Manuela and Londoño, Ernesto. "'License to Kill': Inside Rio's Record Year of Police Killings." *The New York Times*. May 18, 2020. https://www.nytimes.com/2020/05/18/world/americas/brazil-rio-police-violence.html

9   Comissão Parlamentar de Inquérito. *Relatório Final da Comissão Parlamentar de Inquérito Destinada a Investigar a Ação de Milícias no Âmbito do Estado do Rio de Janeiro* [*Final Parliamentary Commission Report on the Actions of Militias in the State of Rio de Janeiro*]. Rio de Janeiro: Legislative Assembly of the State of Rio de Janeiro, 2008.

10 Fogo Cruzado, GENI-UFF, NEV-USP, Pista News, and Disque Denúncia. *Mapa dos Grupos Armados do Rio de Janeiro* [*Map of Armed Groups in Rio de Janeiro*]. Rio de Janeiro, 2020. https://nev.prp.usp.br/mapa-dos-grupos-armados-do-rio-de-janeiro/

11 Instituto de Segurança Pública. *Letalidade Violenta* [*Lethal Violence*]. Rio de Janeiro, March, 2020. http://www.ispdados.rj.gov.br/Arquivos/SeriesHistoricasLetalidadeViolenta.pdf

12 Tate, Julie, Jennifer Jenkins, and Steven Rich. "Fatal Force." *The Washington Post.* August 10, 2020. https://www.washingtonpost.com/graphics/2019/national/police-shootings-2019/

13 Acebes, César Muñoz. *"Good Cops Are Afraid": The Toll of Unchecked Police Violence in Rio de Janeiro.* New York, NY: Human Rights Watch, 2016. https://www.hrw.org/report/2016/07/07/good-cops-are-afraid/toll-unchecked-police-violence-rio-de-janeiro; Delgado, Fernando Ribeiro. *Lethal Force: Police Violence and Public Security in Rio de Janeiro and São Paulo.* New York: Human Rights Watch, 2009. https://www.hrw.org/report/2009/12/08/lethal-force-police-violence-and-public-security-rio-de-janeiro-and-sao-paulo

14 Maia, Gustavo. "'Os caras vão morrer na rua igual barata, pô,' diz Bolsonaro sobre criminosos." ["'They're Going to Die like Cockroaches,' Says Bolsonaro about Criminals"]. *O Globo.* August 5, 2019. https://oglobo.globo.com/brasil/os-caras-vao-morrer-na-rua-igual-barata-po-diz-bolsonaro-sobre-criminosos-23855554

15 "Está sendo destruída a Favelinha de Bonsucesso." *A Noite*, 4, November 24, 1947.; Vieira, 1998, p. 44.

16 Santos, 1983, pp. 7–8.

17 Ribeiro da Silva, 2006, pp. 190–192.

18 Sousa Silva, Eliana. *Testemunhos da Maré* [*Maré Testimonies*] (2nd edition). Rio de Janeiro: Mórula, 2015 [2012], p. 25.

19 "Polícia Civil divulga lista de dez mortos em operação do Bope na Favela Nova Holanda" ["Civil police publishes list of 10 persons killed in BOPE operation in Nova Holanda Favela"]. *Extra.* June 26, 2013. http://extra.globo.com/casos-de-policia/policia-civil-divulga-lista-de-dez-mortos-em-operacao-do-bope-na-favela-nova-holanda-8824548.html

20 Gomes, Marcelo. "Dilma autoriza Exército no Complexo da Maré no Rio" ["Dilma authorizes the entrance of Armed Forces in the Maré Complex in Rio"]. *Exame.* March 29, 2014. https://exame.com/brasil/dilma-autoriza-exercito-no-complexo-da-mare-no-rio/

21 Jesus, 2014.

22 Brito, Diana. "Moradores do Rio denunciam supostos abusos de militares na Maré" ["Rio Residents Denounce Alleged Abuses by the Military in Maré"]. *Folha de São Paulo.* November 5, 2014. http://www1.folha.uol.com.br/cotidiano/2014/11/1543902-moradores-do-rio-denunciam-supostos-abusos-de-militares-na-mare.shtml

23 Viana, Natalia. "Exército é acusado de matar inocentes em operações de segurança pública" ["Army is Accused of Killing Innocent People in Public Security Operations"]. *Pública*. October 31, 2018. https://apublica.org/2018/10/exercito-e-acusado-de-matar-inocentes-em-operacoes-de-seguranca-publica/

24 Sousa Silva, Eliana. *A Ocupação da Maré pelo Exército Brasileiro* [*The Occupation of Maré by the Brazilian Armed Forces*]. Rio de Janeiro: Redes da Maré, 2017, p. 78. https://www.redesdamare.org.br/media/livros/Livro_Pesquisa_ExercitoMare_Maio2017.pdf

25 Redes da Maré. *Direito à Segurança Pública na Maré No. 4* [*The Right to Public Security in Maré No. 4*]. Rio de Janeiro: Redes da Maré, 2019. https://www.redesdamare.org.br/media/downloads/arquivos/BoletimSegPublica_2019.pdf

CHAPTER 4

1 Newhall, Beaumont. *The History of Photography*. New York: Museum of Modern Art, 1982 [1937].

2 Simpson, Audra. "The State is a Man: Theresa Spence, Loretta Saunders and the Gender of Settler Sovereignty." *Theory & Event* 19(4), 2016.

3 Nunes, Georgina Helena Lima. "Lideranças Negras, Terra e Educação em Quilombos" ["Black Leadership, Land, and Education in Quilombos"]. In *Pedagogias populares e epistemologias feministas latino-americanas*, edited by Márcia Alves da Silva and Graziela Rinaldi da Rosa. Curitiba BR: Brazil Publishing, 139-154, 2019.

4 Rui, Taniele. "Por entre Territórios Visíveis e Territórios Invisibilizados: Mercados ilícitos e cracolândias de São Paulo e Rio de Janeiro" ["In-between Visible and Invisibilized Territories: Illicit Markets and Cracolândias in São Paulo and Rio de Janeiro"]. *Novos estudos CEBRAP* 38(3), 573–588, 2019.

CHAPTER 5

1 Smith, Christen. "Lingering Trauma in Brazil: Police Violence against Black Women." *NACLA — Report on the Americas 50* (4), 369-377, 2018.

2 da Costa Bezerra, Kátia. *Postcards from Rio: Favelas and the Contested Geographies of Citizenship*. New York, NY: Fordham University Press, 2017.

3 Larkins, Erika Robb. *The Spectacular Favela: Violence in Modern Brazil*. Berkeley, CA: University of California Press, 2015.

CHAPTER 6

1. Valladares, Licia do Prado. *The Invention of the Favela*. Trans. Robert N. Anderson. Chapel Hill, NC: University of North Carolina Press, 2019, p. xv.

2. Valladares, 2019, p. 145.

3. Orr, Gregory. *Poetry as Survival*. Athens, GA: University of Georgia Press, 2002, p. 16.

4. Orr, 2002, p. 47.

5. Marcuse, Herbert. *The Aesthetic Dimension*. Boston, MA: Beacon Press Books, 1978, p. 41.

6. Freire, Paulo. *Pedagogy of the Oppressed*. New York, NY: Herder & Herder, 1970.

7. De Certeau, Michel, *The Practice of Everyday Life*. Trans. Steven Rendall. Berkeley, CA: University of California Press, 1984.

8. Blauvelt, Andrew, "Strangely Familiar: Design in Everyday Life." In *Strangely Familiar: Design and Everyday Life* edited by Andrew Blauvelt. Minneapolis, MN: Walker Art Center, 2003, p. 20.

CONCLUSION

1. Bauman, Zygmunt. *Strangers at our Door*. Cambridge, UK: Polity Press, 2016, pp. 82–83.

2. Santos Junior, Orlando Alves and Patrícia Ramos Novaes. "Impactos socioespaciais do experimento neoliberal na cidade do Rio de Janeiro no contexto dos Jogos Olímpicos de 2016" ["Sociospatial Impacts of the Neoliberal Experiment in the City of Rio de Janeiro in the Context of the 2016 Olympic Games"]. In *Militarização no Rio de Janeiro: Da pacificação à intervenção* ["Militarization in Rio de Janeiro: From Pacification to Intervention"], edited by Leite, Márcia Pereira, Lia de Mattos Rocha, Juliana Farias, and Monique Batista Carvalho. Rio de Janeiro: Mórula, 17-38, 2018.

3. Harvey, David. *A Brief History of Neoliberalism*. Oxford, UK: Oxford University Press, 2007.

4. Leite, Márcia Pereira, Lia de Mattos Rocha, Juliana Farias, and Monique Batista Carvalho. "Sobre os dispositivos de governo dos pobres em uma cidade militarizada" ["On the dispositives of the government of the

poor in a militarized city"]. In *Militarização no Rio de Janeiro: Da pacificação à intervenção* ["Militarization in Rio de Janeiro: From Pacification to Intervention"], edited by Márcia Pereira Leite, Lia de Mattos Rocha, Juliana Farias, and Monique Batista Carvalho. Rio de Janeiro: Mórula, 9-16, 2018.

5   Bauman, 2016, p. 29.

6   Spinoza, Benedictus de. Ethics. Trans. Robert Harvey Monro Elwes. Digireads.com Publishing, 2019, V.III.

7   Frankl, Viktor E. *Man's Search for Meaning*. Boston, MA: Beacon Press, 2014 [1959], p. 78.

Made in the USA
Columbia, SC
20 May 2021